The Alchemy of

The Alchemy of Innovation

Perspectives from the leading edge

Alan Barker

First published in 2002 by
Spiro Press
Robert Hyde House
48 Bryanston Square
London W1H 2EA
Telephone: +44 (0)20 7479 2000

ISBN 1 904298 01 X

British Library Cataloguing-in-Publication Data.
A catalogue record for this book is available from the British Library.

Spiro Press USA
3 Front Street, Suite 331
PO Box 338
Rollinsford, NH 03869
USA

Typeset by: Wyvern 21 Ltd, Bristol
Printed in Great Britain by: The Cromwell Press
Cover image by: Digital Vision
Cover design by: Sign Design

Foreword

I have spent my life looking at everyday objects and trying to innovate; to rethink their design and technology from first principles.

One Saturday in 1978 I was vacuuming at home with an old, bag vacuum cleaner. It wasn't sucking very well, so I took the machine to bits to see how it worked – or didn't. That's when I realized the fundamental problem with bag vacuum cleaners: they clog with dust, which chokes the airflow and decimates suction power.

I started to think about a different way of trapping the dust that wouldn't clog the machine. I had recently installed an industrial cyclone, for collecting paint dust, in the factory where I worked. I began to think about using the same cyclone concept in a domestic vacuum cleaner. It took me five years, building over 5,000 prototypes, until I had perfected the Dual Cyclone™ technology.

I then spent a further two years trawling the UK and Europe with my technology hoping that someone would want to license it, with no success. I distinctly remember the head of one large company telling me that 'If there was a better way of making vacuum cleaners then someone else would have invented it before now.' These big, complacent companies were not interested in a new and better solution.

The only way forward was to try and manufacture the cleaner myself. I gathered a small team of young engineering designers, fresh from the Royal College of Art, and we started working in the old coach house behind the house where I lived.

Together we set about developing a Dual Cyclone™ vacuum cleaner for the British market, funded in part by a Japanese licence and eventually by borrowing $1 million from the bank.

We launched DCO1 in 1993. Two years later, it was the best selling vacuum cleaner in the UK. By simply, and solely, striving to create new and better products we have, as a result, created a substantial company.

Today, our creative teams in engineering and research remain the core of the company. However, we constantly need to strive for innovation. This led us to consider the domestic washing machine; its inefficiencies and sheer inability to get clothes really clean.

During our research we discovered that 15 minutes of handwashing produced cleaner clothing than the 67 minute washing cycle of the most advanced and best performing washing machine. Our task was to find a technology that replicated the action of handwashing.

At one stage we were experimenting with a paddle that knocked the clothes down to the bottom of the drum, which meant that we had to split the drum in two. On impulse we tried running these two aligned drums in opposite directions and were amazed at the results: even better than handwashing. We had created a bigger, faster, more efficient washing machine.

The Contrarotator™ uses better and different technology; its development shows our fundamental approach. There was the need for significant improvement, and it was the capacity for constant observation that mattered in the end.

If you want to make a product with a big difference you have to work differently. Everyone who starts work at Dyson makes a vacuum cleaner, be they in production or engineering. Then they can take it home and use it. In this way they become customers of their own product: they understand it and the reason why the company exists.

Dyson would like all its employees to do things differently, almost just for the sake of it, constantly forcing them to think through every move. This isn't some management gimmick – it is fundamental to the way we develop new products. People are encouraged to take risks and if they make mistakes then, so what? Mistakes are what you learn from.

I don't think it is enough to 'build a better mousetrap'. Commercial success comes from understanding why it is better, and why people need a better one. When Percy Shaw invented the cat's eye in 1934, subsequently used all over the world, he didn't just get lucky by having a good idea. Yes he invented it, but he also had the acumen and foresight to choose to invent it. We shouldn't separate out the inventive act from having an understanding of people, of the market. It's this combination that leads to commercial success. That is what you might call innovation.

James Dyson, practising engineer and Chairman of Dyson

Contents

Introduction

Think of this book as a journey of exploration.

'Innovation' is the word of the moment. No organization wants to be seen as anything but innovative. But what do we mean when we use this word? What do senior managers refer to, precisely, when they talk about 'releasing the creativity of people at work'?

I have always seen work as fundamentally creative: all work, not just the work we normally call 'creative'. Work, at its best, is about making something that has not previously existed: a new product or a new service perhaps, but also a tidy filing system, an efficient invoicing procedure, a clean floor. Yet something about work in organizations discourages us from thinking about work like this. Most managers would surely agree that creativity is a good idea; but few find the opportunity to exercise creativity in their own work. And many of us find work more or less boring or frustrating as a result.

It is partly a problem of design. We don't structure organizations to support creativity. We create them, by and large, to do the same thing, over and over again, as well as possible. Consistency and reliability; these are what we want from the organizations that we use as customers, and from the organizations that employ us. Small wonder, then, that senior managers are reluctant to heed the management gurus' calls to 'innovate or die'. Survey after survey suggests that managers see innovation as a desirable strategic objective; yet the same surveys invariably show that few organizations innovate systematically. To innovate means to change, to take risks, to step outside known territory. A paradox: we desire change *and* we desire stability. How can we achieve both?

Other questions rapidly follow. Where are the wellsprings of innovation? Are there organizing principles of innovation? Is any initiative that creates change in an organization innovative? Or does a change programme have to have some particular outcome to count as innovation? And, deep down, there is another question: Is innovation not somehow related to the very nature of work itself? Might an investigation of this elusive topic reveal something about how we work in organizations, and how we might work together more creatively?

I have become deeply interested in innovation over the past 12 years. My background in training led me naturally towards the skills and techniques that have been developed to help people innovate; but I have also become intrigued by the processes by which innovation happens and the organizational climate or culture in which it happens.

Now, in a global situation of rapidly increasing uncertainty, it seems obvious to me that innovation is not merely desirable but *vital* to our future. Yet – although our ability to innovate arguably defines us as human beings – we seem to be pitifully unsophisticated in our approach to it. In particular, we find it enormously difficult to innovate in groups or organizations.

Innovation is too important an activity to be left to the maverick entrepreneurs and social visionaries. We must find ways of innovating *together*. The burning question is: How can we organize ourselves to innovate?

We set up a conference to address this question. This book was born out of that conference. We decided on the name 'The Alchemy of Innovation'. The name was in some ways an obvious choice. Innovation results from a rich mix of activities: strategic planning, research and development (R&D), marketing, project management, teamwork, training, creative thinking. I wanted to reflect innovation's multi-dimensional quality. For the conference, I gathered a group of speakers with direct, practical experience in these diverse approaches.

The word 'alchemy' seemed, too, to encapsulate our passionate desire to find the key to innovation: the philosopher's stone that might somehow magically – and consistently – turn the lead of daily toil into the gold of creativity. Many writers give the impression that there might be some secret formula that will produce innovation in organizations, whatever the circumstances. Indeed, many of those drawn to the conference may have been in search of just such a formula. By using the word 'alchemy', we were able to draw attention to that quest for an all-embracing answer, and to challenge it.

But the word seemed well chosen for another, more metaphorical, reason.

Alchemy was a science of correspondences. Alchemists sought similarities between the workings of the heavens and those of the earth – and, indeed, of human beings. These correspondences were evidence, to the alchemists, of a grand design in the universe, of a divine imagination that needed only to be decoded to be understood. Alchemists' attempts to crack the codes led directly to mathematics (for many of the correspondences were numerical) and, more obscurely, to experimental science.

Over the centuries, alchemy fell into disrepute. Thinkers in the late European Renaissance began to suspect that all these correspondences might be merely the product of the alchemists' imagination. The scientific revolution of the 17th century – the revolution that laid the intellectual foundations for the Industrial Revolution a century later – systematically removed these fanciful constructions in favour of observation and experiment. Modern chemistry, for example, could be seen as alchemy stripped of imagination. The new scientists came to look on the universe not as an imaginative creation, but as an intricate machine. They saw alchemists as little more than magicians, weaving spells of their own invention. Worse; they were charlatans, gulling the credulous with false ideas – and impossible promises.

For alchemy had been an applied science. Alchemists sought to use their knowledge for mankind's benefit. They sought practical solutions to urgent problems. Alchemy was a science of transmutation, a discipline of change. There were obvious benefits in turning lead into gold. But alchemists also yearned to transform old age into youth and sickness into health (a good deal of medicine has its roots in this ancient science). Alchemy was indeed magic; and it was *practical* magic.

Innovation seems to share some important characteristics with alchemy. It, too, is a discipline of change. It, too, seeks to create something new, and something of use. And the processes that result in innovations seem often to be mysterious or magical. They are imaginative and associative. Creativity is often explained as thinking that seeks correspondences between elements from unrelated spheres of experience. When they meet in our imagination, the resultant 'spark' is a new idea. By imagining a process, a product or a business relationship *in terms of* other processes or objects or relationships, we find new ways of thinking about them.

Our models of organizations, of course, derive from the science and technology that superseded alchemy. They are fundamentally mechanical. We continue to organize work, and workers, in much the same way that an engineer might organize the parts of a machine. In the two hundred and more years since the Industrial Revolution, we have designed organizations functionally and turned people into functionaries.

In this context, innovation comes to look very much like any other industrial process. It is the creation of new products – often high technology machines. The work is often organized as a kind of assembly line, from initial idea to product launch.

For some years, this industrial metaphor has come under fire, not merely for dehumanizing workplaces but also for misrepresenting organizational work. Some of us saw business process reengineering (BPR) – popularized by Hammer and Champy in their influential book *Reengineering the Corporation* – as a last gasp of the industrial metaphor. The alchemists of management are now looking elsewhere for their metaphors. They are looking to biology and to the new sciences of complexity and quantum mechanics. These sciences seem to offer a closer analogy to the complex organizations and networks in which we work, and their turbulent, unpredictable environment.

In this new world view, innovation looks less mechanical and more organic. It is less a process of assembly than of evolution, less industrial and more cognitive: a process that involves the intelligent use of knowledge and the capacity to learn. The new paradigms of innovation are systemic and cyclical rather than mechanistic and linear. They emphasize change, contingency and the dynamics of people working together. These are the paradigms that delineate the new landscape of innovation.

This book, then, is an imaginative journey. Each chapter takes us into a different part of the landscape. You might see it also as an extended dialogue. My own chapters are interposed with others written by people whose direct experience of innovation yields valuable insights. They accepted my invitation to speak at the conference, and then to put their ideas into writing. I am grateful to them all for their hard work, without which this book would be far the poorer.

We begin with definitions – staking out the ground and relating innovation to the wider aspects of our lives in organizations.

- **Chapter 1.** What do we mean by 'innovation'? Can we see our ability to innovate as some defining feature of our humanity? How might it relate to those other key characteristics of human beings – our ability to learn and to co-operate?
- **Chapter 2.** What are the wellsprings of innovation? Can we define creativity? How might we recognize it, or manage it?
- **Chapter 3.** What are the environments in which innovation flourishes? What might an innovative culture look like? Where have innovative cultures developed? What characterizes them? Can we recreate such cultures deliberately? Do organizational cultures have the same characteristics as wider social cultures?

We then move on to look at managing innovation within organizations, at both the organizational and the team level.

- **Chapter 4.** How does innovation fit within broader strategies of organizations? Can we systematize innovation into manageable processes? What might such processes look like? Which are the most effective?
- **Chapter 5.** What are the 'hard' and 'soft' elements of innovation management? Sarah Lloyd-Jones of Unilever offers an intriguing perspective on the forces and stresses at work in innovation teams.

- **Chapter 6.** Does innovation progress in a straight line or in cycles? Kevin Byron of Nortel Networks provides a valuable insight into the complexities of innovation management in telecommunications.
- **Chapter 7.** How do we manage the innovators? How might we put together teams to innovate? What skills will the team need? How do we foster them? Are there examples of successful innovation management – in the arts, for example?

The last section of the book looks at innovation from a cognitive perspective. Innovation, more than any other organizational activity, demands high quality thinking. In this section, we investigate what characterizes that thinking and how we might encourage it.

- **Chapter 8.** What does it mean to train creativity? How to relate such training to other innovation initiatives? Gillian Barker challenges trainers to gain a deeper understanding of what they do when they introduce the skills of creativity into organizations.
- **Chapter 9.** How does innovation relate to knowledge management (KM)? What do we mean by knowledge? How can we harness the knowledge in our organizations to innovate? Does innovation demand that we manage it as a resource or as a function of behaviour?
- **Chapter 10.** How can we manage knowledge in the pursuit of innovation? Peter Matthews demonstrates how knowledge management has promoted innovation in one of the largest utility companies in the UK – Anglian Water.
- **Afterword.** Finally, we pull the strands together and ask the big question: What is necessary for the alchemy of innovation to take place?

The journey will yield many discoveries. 'Creativity,' said mythographer Joseph Campbell, 'consists in going out to find the thing society hasn't found yet.' In the language of the new information economy, I would be pleased if you saw this book as a 'portal' guiding you on to the next stage of your own journey towards innovation.

What do you mean, 'innovation'?

Few concepts are as hard to pin down as 'innovation'. In its original meaning, of course, it means 'making new' or 'making something new'. But even here, the word is ambiguous: it can mean the process of creating, and also the creation itself.

The word has become ubiquitous. In different contexts, it can take on radically different meanings.

- Innovation can refer to the **process of introducing new products** – usually involving more or less high technology. In this context, it can often become confused with invention. We might distinguish the two by saying that an invention becomes an innovation only when it is introduced into the market. The same invention might lead to different innovations. The refrigerator, for example, is a useful invention. As a device for keeping food fresh, it has proved a highly successful innovation; but the apocryphal salesman who sold refrigerators to the Inuit as a means of stopping their food from freezing solid created another innovation from the same invention.
- The word can also explain the **method** by which such new products are created: many models seek to systematize the innovation process. Within that process, the word might become at times almost interchangeable with 'creativity'.
- Innovation can be institutionalized as the **name of an organizational function**, the exclusive responsibility of a department. The definition

can expand to cover a strategy, at which point it may become indistinguishable from 'change management'.

- In the mouth of a politician, innovation can be some **vague social benefit**, a self-recommending good that all parts of society should strive for.
- If we were to look into other disciplines – anthropology, palaeontology – innovation appears as a **defining characteristic** of our humanity.

Let's start with a simple definition: *Innovation is creating new sources of customer satisfaction.*

It introduces and *applies* ideas, not merely within an organization but in its environment. The application is something that a customer can recognize: a product or a service. Its newness and value as an innovation are in the eye of the customer, not of the innovator.

CREATIVITY AND INNOVATION – A MARRIAGE OF CONVENIENCE?

The words 'creativity' and 'innovation' often crop up together. If you want one, apparently, you must have the other. Indeed, from the way corporate language uses the two words – in annual reports, job advertisements, vision and mission statements and the like – we might suspect that they are one and the same thing. There is a real danger that they blur into a single, vague, 'catch all' concept: something self-evidently desirable (who would want to work for an organization that was neither creative nor innovative?), but not entirely well defined.

We need to distinguish the two terms. We already have a definition of innovation. Here is a similarly tentative definition of creativity: *Creativity is the ability to generate new ideas.*

Innovation is a process; creativity is the set of skills or aptitudes that makes the process possible. Creativity is the (predominantly mental) activity that results in innovation; an innovation is the tangible or outward result of creativity.

We shall examine creativity in more detail in Chapter 2. For now, we might simply note that we can distinguish between the two broadly in structural terms. Creativity is generally regarded as individualistic and somewhat capricious: hard to define and harder to manage. Innovation, in contrast, is usually seen as a structured group process, offering economic or market advantage. Government departments, for example, are more enthusiastic about supporting research into innovation than into creativity. Senior managers are more likely to be interested in a consultant offering to increase their capacity to innovate, than in a project seeking to release people's creative potential. Creativity is all very well, it seems; but it is innovation that offers the real rewards.

PETER DRUCKER AND SYSTEMATIC INNOVATION

Peter Drucker has written long and wisely about innovation. He defines it as 'the act that endows resources with a new capacity to create wealth.' With typically uncompromising clarity, he recognizes that innovation is not the management of change, but the purposeful *search* for changes that an enterprise can exploit. He links innovation with the entrepreneur, whom he defines as someone who searches for change and exploits it as an opportunity. 'Innovation,' says Drucker, 'is the specific instrument of entrepreneurship.' But he goes further. He sees innovation as one of the central reasons for any organization to exist.

A commercial enterprise, Drucker says, has two, and only two, functions: to innovate and to market. All of its other activities are costs. Because he sees innovation as a core activity for any enterprise, Drucker is keen to elevate it into a discipline: a systematic process that is not subject to the vagaries of imagination.

Drucker's book, *Innovation and Entrepreneurship*, is a thorough examination of seven sources of innovative opportunity. He makes it plain that their order is not arbitrary. They are listed 'in descending order of reliability and predictability'. The systematic innovator won't waste time on new knowledge or hunches about swings in the market when they could search out the unexpected successes or failures of the last few months. These opportunities present relatively low risk and uncertainty.

SEVEN SOURCES OF OPPORTUNITY

Drucker outlines seven main sources of innovative opportunity.

The first four sets of opportunities lie within the business or its market sector.

1 *The unexpected* – the unforeseen success or failure; the unprecedented outside event.
2 *The incongruity* – between what is and what ought to be, between reality and our assumptions about it.
3 *Process need* – a process becomes inefficient or ineffective and needs to change.
4 *Changes in industry or market structure*.

The last three lie outside the enterprise itself.

5 *Demographics* – changes in population.
6 *Changes in perception* – mood swings or new reasoning in society at large.
7 *New knowledge* – scientific, social or otherwise.

Drucker demonstrates that innovation is as much social as technological. Many of the most influential innovations of the last two centuries, he points out, have been social rather than technical: merchant banking, the modern university, mail-order retailing, integrated health services. They have also been achieved socially: their success has been the result of people working together.

This last is a vitally important point. It challenges one of our deepest assumptions about innovation: that it is the preserve of the heroic individualist.

THE MAVERICK MYTH

Talk of innovation and you probably soon find yourself talking of mavericks. Peter Drucker may paint a picture of innovation as a strategic discipline; but most of us see innovation as the province of the maverick individualist. We tend to associate innovation with subversive activity, radical insight and reckless bravado. This is 'innovation against all odds'; and it needs a hero.

He is 'The Maverick'. He – very often 'he' – is wildly imaginative, dreamy, revolutionary in his outlook. He dares to ask the questions others ignore; he stumbles on chance discoveries or works on hunches; he pursues his dream with fanatical enthusiasm, often against impossible odds, to be vindicated at last as his innovation triumphs commercially or socially.

The Maverick is an entrepreneur. As heroic innovator, he first appears in the work of the Austrian economist, Joseph Schumpeter. Schumpeter had lived through a world of turbulent and unpredictable change; his theory of innovation is correspondingly violent. The entrepreneur, according to Schumpeter, brings about 'a gale of creative destruction.' Before Schumpeter, the entrepreneur co-ordinated resources; by contrast, Schumpeter sees him *creating* resources. He stumbles, either accidentally or after searching, on gold-bearing rock; the conversion of gold then leads to the development of infrastructure: roads, guides, services, systems of exchange and contract. This two-stage process – discovery followed by diffusion or exploitation – characterizes Schumpeter's model of entrepreneurial innovation.

The myth of the heroic innovator has been remarkably persistent. Many books about innovation repeat the stories of innovators making their mark against the odds (including James Dyson's autobiography!) – and often against the grain of their own backgrounds. John Boyd Dunlop, the inventor of the pneumatic tyre, was a veterinarian; Laszlo Biro, inventor of the ballpoint pen, was a sculptor. Automatic telephone dialling was developed by Almon B Strowger, an undertaker; photocopying was invented by Chester Carlson, a lawyer. Such heroes of innovation often seize the opportunity offered by the mistake, the failure or the experiment gone wrong. Alistair Pilkington discovered the process for producing float glass after a machine broke. Polyethylene was invented after a pressure vessel started leaking. The Post-It note was famously the outcome of a glue formulation that failed to be sufficiently sticky. These are the stories that get repeated. What is not so often mentioned is that, without organized work, these inventions would never have become innovations at all.

Innovation is too important to be left to the mavericks. Undoubtedly, it often takes an outstanding individual to recognize an opportunity and risk all to exploit it. Yet the myth – and I use the word with care, to suggest the power that this image has over our attitude to work and to innovation – offers only a partial explanation of how innovation works. An idea may only ever be the product of a single mind, but implementing it will always demand working with others. Innovation is a social phenomenon. It finds its expression within society; and it takes collaborative activity to make it happen.

THE ORIGINS OF INNOVATION

If innovation is not the province of the isolated creative, where might we find its roots? Could any of us be innovators? Is there, perhaps, something in our very humanity that makes us naturally innovative?

Steven Mithen is an archaeologist with a particular interest in the origins of human intelligence. In his book, *The Prehistory of the Mind*, Mithen examines what we know of human evolution for clues to our peculiar and – as far as we know – unique ability to innovate. It's a fragmented story; the evidence is sparse and often open to contradictory interpretations. Mithen pieces together what he can and attempts to make sense of the fragments by comparing them to models of the mind's architecture that have been developed by psychologists.

Mithen suggests that a small number of factors distinguish our mental activity from that of other animals. For example, both humans and chimps live in complex social groups. Both are highly intelligent and display the ability to solve problems. But humans, in Mithen's view, exhibit three mental characteristics that have never been observed in chimps.

- **We can learn.** We can accumulate knowledge gradually over time and adapt our thinking to new knowledge. We can also reflect upon the contents of our own minds.
- **We can think creatively.** We are able to improve on solutions, combine elements of our thinking and generate new ideas.
- **We can think collaboratively.** Our sophisticated use of language allows us to swap ideas and work on problems in teams.

Each of these three mental characteristics has its part to play in innovation. Their absence in an otherwise highly intelligent animal like a chimpanzee may help to explain why we can innovate, and they can't.

Chimps find it almost impossible to learn more than a very little. Much publicized projects to teach chimpanzees language seem to proclaim more spectacular success than they have actually achieved. Researchers have been able to teach only a limited vocabulary and the barest rudiments of grammar to chimps; significantly, the animals involved have rarely if ever used what they have learned to express more than the simplest and most immediate desires.

More crucially, chimps cannot make use of their learning. As learners, they are individualists: we have little evidence of social learning and even less of teaching among chimps. A youngster might imitate the actions of an older animal in using a stick to draw termites out of a tree; but there's no real evidence that a learned skill is consciously transmitted through the group, or that groups communicate ideas between them.

So chimp learning has to start afresh with each new generation, and in each new group. Chimps face the same problems over and over again. In Mithen's words, they live in a universe that is 'static, constrained and highly personalized.'

A yet more radical distinction between humans and chimps is in our attitudes to problems. Humans love problem solving for its own sake. Mithen paints a vivid picture of this energetic curiosity, this in-built urge to *look for* problems, that characterizes the human mind: a mind 'so restless, so inquiring, so desperate to acquire knowledge.'

Our capacity to communicate is vital to innovation, too. To observe a young chimp and a young human at play is to contemplate two utterly different mental activities.

I remember playing with my daughter when she was 18 months old, on the verge of complex speech and already a competent walker. The patterns of play might be quite similar; but nothing a chimp does – or will ever be able to do – could compare to my daughter's inventiveness, to the sheer delight in making a new discovery or exercising a new skill. But what struck me most forcibly was her skill in communicating: to show and to demonstrate. Everyone who has played with a toddler will know their love of *giving* things to others, apparently for no other reason than to share their discovery. If only adults were as unselfish with their knowledge!

But it's our ability to learn that seems to make the biggest difference. Young children seem to be programmed with a compulsive *desire* to learn (though not always what we might want them to learn), and to try out new ideas. As a child grows, however, its mind achieves something even more remarkable. Its long-term memory is far more powerful than any chimp's. Not only can we remember what we have discovered; we can also *make use* of our own thoughts.

The human mind, alone in the natural world, can act on *its own contents*. Our ability to think about our own thinking makes the human mind unimaginably flexible and creative. Human beings can learn. And the capacity to learn grants us the capacity to innovate.

It seems, then, that innovation is a defining characteristic of our humanity. How did we come to gain such a capacity?

THE EVOLUTION OF CREATIVITY

Homo sapiens did not, apparently, innovate immediately. Human culture doesn't develop for tens of thousands of years after the species appears. But, when new ideas do appear, they come thick and fast. Archaeologists are fond of describing a 'cultural explosion' in the history of mankind. It occurred between 60,000 and 30,000 years ago – a relatively short period in our evolutionary history. In fact, the 'explosion' is a set of different innovations, in different parts of the world. Australia was colonized about 60,000 years ago, using boats. New tool technology appears in the Middle East around 50-45,000 years ago; the first art objects in Europe 40,000 years ago. It is as if a number of gates have been opened; once unlocked, the stream of innovations becomes endless and unstoppable.

Inevitably, the archaeological record emphasizes technology. We began to make multi-component tools, from a range of materials: wood, bone, ivory. We began to vary the design of our tools, and to design specific tools for hunting specific animals. All of these are striking innovations, never before seen in human history.

And we began to create art. Objects of personal adornment appear around 40,000 years ago; painting and carving appear around 30,000 years ago. We painted our caves with elegant images of ourselves and other animals. The artistic skill with which we created these images sprang fully formed into existence. We were also playing music: flutes have been discovered, made of eagle bone. These innovations are more than developments of skill or technical application; they imply the growth of complex social relationships and networks. Little female statuettes, known as 'Venus figurines', were carried throughout Europe and Russia; humans were operating alliance networks across huge distances: collaboration on a grand scale.

Why did these events occur? Mithen's explanation is intriguing: it builds an architecture of the mind that may help us to understand how we innovate – and, therefore, how we might manage innovation more effectively.

MENTAL ARCHITECTURE

Mithen proposes that the human mind is like a cathedral. Like other cathedrals, it has developed over time. Its history, he suggests, has three broad phases.

In **phase one**, the mind, in its earliest form, consists only of a central 'nave': a general intelligence that is adept at simple problem solving and applying a limited range of techniques. This general intelligence is much like that of chimps.

In **phase two**, the mind acquires a number of specialized intelligences (or 'cognitive domains') that are like 'chapels' surrounding the 'nave'. Mithen posits three:

- a *social intelligence* that helps us to understand relationships and predict others' behaviour;
- a *technical intelligence* that helps us to manipulate objects and make new ones; and
- a *natural history intelligence*, by which we relate to animals, plants and other parts of nature.

In this second phase, Mithen suggests that we were able to use these different kinds of intelligence separately, but not to combine them. Ideas about social relationships and ideas about tools, for example, develop separately and without any cognitive connection. This is the kind of mind that early humans may have possessed. Our mental cathedral had a central nave and a number of separate chapels, but thick walls separated the various sections of the building.

In **phase three**, Mithen suggests that doors or windows open up between the 'chapels' of the mind, so that the contents of one part become available to another. We gain 'cognitive fluidity'; the ability to combine ideas from different parts of the mind or view the contents of one part with the mental models of another. This cognitive fluidity is at the root of the cultural explosion – and, by implication, of our ability to innovate.

THE MIND AS A CATHEDRAL

Mithen gives a number of powerful examples of the innovations resulting from this new-found cognitive fluidity.

- Art, for example, combines natural history intelligence with technical intelligence. Using the former, we can interpret the signs of natural activity; using the latter, we can create objects from mental templates.

The two abilities, combined, produce a work of art.

- Combining art with social intelligence makes objects of personal adornment possible: artistic designs that express social status and power.
- Combine natural history intelligence and technical intelligence and we can suddenly produce new tools for hunting specific prey.
- Combine natural history intelligence with social intelligence and we produce anthropomorphism: the ability to imagine animals as people (and *vice versa*). This allows us then to predict animal behaviour and hunt more efficiently.

It's a persuasive idea. Innovation is the result of a specific mental alchemy: our ability to combine different *kinds* of intelligence to produce new ideas, new solutions to problems, new technology and new forms of social and cultural interaction. The idea may also explain why innovations occurred – and often continue to occur – so unexpectedly. That 'Aha!' moment of discovery is a 'door' suddenly swinging open between two mental domains.

Mithen's model can also explain why creativity is sometimes so difficult – particularly when groups of people are trying to think together. Humans are still mental specialists. We develop 'cognitive domains' for different parts of our thinking – for most of us, many more than three! We sometimes find it hard to make intelligent connections between these specialisms. Different mental elements work away at their own problems, like so many 'cubicle workers'. We may endure long periods being 'stuck' in one cognitive domain before a hole is suddenly and mysteriously punched in the wall that gives us insight into another part of the cathedral. To solve problems outside these 'chapels of the mind' – social problems, problems involving great complexity or ambiguity – we often resort to the kind of primitive, generalized intelligence that inhabits the ancient, central 'nave' of our minds.

This mental architecture is reflected in our organizational structures. We build our organizations out of functional specialisms that often find it hard to talk to one another. The alchemy of innovation arises from breaking down the mental and organizational walls that limit our thinking.

AGRICULTURE – THE FIRST CASE STUDY IN INNOVATION?

Agriculture is perhaps the most important innovation in human history. It changed human society more radically than any other innovation, before or since.

No one knows quite why it happened. For over 200,000 years, humans were hunter-gatherers. Then, about 10,000 years ago, something odd happened: we started to settle down. There was no obvious reason for doing so: agriculture, initially, actually *lowers* standards of health in a population.

So why did we do it? It may have been a response to intense global warming. About 10,000 years ago, the Earth seems to have undergone a period of intense global warming, more dramatic than anything we currently fear: average temperatures rose by some seven degrees centigrade *in a decade*. The results for ecosystems must have been catastrophic.

Humans responded to the crisis by starting to plant crops and raise animals for food. Imagine how *strange* this idea must have been at first. Hunter-gatherers start to plant and cultivate; they herd animals rather than simply hunting them. As a solution to an impending disaster, agriculture is as peculiar as it is brilliant.

Agriculture demands cognitive fluidity. Crop production demands the ability to think of living things as objects to manipulate. Keeping animals demands the combination of natural history and social intelligences, being able to care for animals as we would our own children.

But agriculture also illustrates innovation's recurring habit of proceeding in cycles – or spirals. Innovative solutions typically create new problems, more complicated than those solved by the initial innovation. Cultivating crops and domesticating animals, for example, both demand new skills and forms of collaboration.

Success in food production generates a surplus: what to do with the leftovers? The answer: innovate a form of exchange – trade. Trade itself demands new specialisms and forms of contract. People need to meet regularly; we begin to gather into bustling villages and towns.

Such communities bring yet more problems. How to solve social disputes? How to maintain hygiene? How to replenish the fertility of the land? How to gain raw materials and distribute the wealth created by the community?

Agriculture spawned new challenges and new innovations that were as much social and economic as technological. The development of social divisions, political structures, trading networks and administration all arose from the problems posed by agriculture.

LANGUAGE – THE LIBERATOR OF INNOVATIVE THINKING

How did the first cultural explosion occur? What punched the holes in the walls of our specialized intelligences? And what allows us to go on innovating? An alternative version of phase three in the mind's evolution posits a new cognitive domain: a 'superchapel' of the mind in which elements from our specialized intelligences can be combined. Experience and ideas from one specialized area can now influence experience and ideas from another. People can now think in new ways, about new things and new ways of behaving. We gain the ability to think about things *in terms of other things*. We gain the power of metaphor and analogy. And it is this power that lies at the root of our ability to innovate.

But what is the alchemical medium; the crucible in which these new mental compounds appear?

The answer is language. Language apparently originally evolved as a means of exchanging social information. We invented language as a way of creating and maintaining social relationships. Stephen Mithen suggests that, embedded within this primal social language, lay 'snippets' of information about the non-social world: about objects and nature. The people who were able to integrate these snippets into the language and make use of them in new ways gained a competitive advantage over those who couldn't. Bit by bit, language made other specialized intelligences available for use in a single domain. It was language that created the 'super-chapel' where we combine and transform mental material.

Earlier in this chapter, we saw how human thinking has three characteristics that distinguishes it from the mental activity of other animals.

- **Active learning through memory** – our ability to store and re-use knowledge.
- **Creativity** – our ability to create new ideas.
- **Collaboration** – our ability to think in groups.

All three of these characteristics are made possible only through language.

First, language is a storage medium. It allows us to retrieve information more efficiently. Once we have access to a common language, others' knowledge becomes available to us. It also helps us to learn by turning our experience into ideas. We can certainly think without language; but we can't have ideas without it. A potter, for instance, may be able to throw a pot with great skill, but find it hard to explain the process. Only in language can we *conceptualize* our experience. To continue the example, only in language can we define the potter's creation *as a pot*. Being able to think about the *idea* of a pot liberates your thinking about it. If you want to have ideas, you have to have language.

Language also gives us the power of creativity. It gives our imagination greater power by allowing us to reflect on the *possibilities* inherent in a situation. Taking our example of the potter still further: with language, we could imagine what the potter creates as a storage vessel, an ornament, a vase, a trophy, food storage, a medium for artistic self-expression, and so on. Language allows us to think about something *in terms of something else*. Language makes metaphor possible. And metaphor is the royal road to innovation.

Finally, language opens the door to collaboration. With a shared language, we can tell others about our ideas, ask them about theirs, and 'put our heads together' to create new ideas. Without language, we remain in the 'static, constrained and highly personalized' universe of the chimpanzee; with it, however, we enter the dynamic, liberated, social universe of human culture.

Language, then, is at the very heart of what we mean by innovation. It is the key that unlocks the chapels of the human mind, allowing us to explore the whole cathedral and use its contents creatively. It allows us to bring mental material into consciousness, reflect on it and manipulate it. It is the means by which we can share our thinking with others and improve the quality of our thinking through collaboration. Innovation happens in language. Our ability to use language effectively, creatively and collaboratively directly affects our skill as innovators.

2

A brief history of creativity

Creativity is the activity that delivers innovation; it is the spark, the well-spring. But just what kind of activity is it? Look through the huge number of books promoting and encouraging creativity, and a single definition is hard to find. Some themes, though, do emerge.

- Creativity is often spoken of as **something 'special'** or out of the ordinary. We may see it as a gift that only certain people possess; it is often associated with the idea of an artistic temperament, or even with mental instability and madness. Consultants and others may try to convince us that anybody can be creative, but that nevertheless it is one of the most remarkable hallmarks of being human. Creativity, seen in this light, is mysterious and magical, resistant to analysis and hard to pin down.
- Creativity is often associated with **thinking or problem solving**. Whatever this quality or process might be, it is usually described as mental: occurring in the mind and associated with ideas. The phrases 'creative thinking' or Edward de Bono's celebrated 'lateral thinking' place creativity firmly within the cognitive realm. Creativity – at least in the self-help books or the corporate arena – is something you do in your head, and is rarely considered in relation to physical activity or work with physical objects.
- Considered as a form of thinking, creativity is often described **in opposition to rationality or logic**. To be creative means to find excep-

tional or unusual ways of thinking about something: to think 'outside the box'. This notion of breaking through the assumptions that constrain 'normal' thinking has provoked a host of techniques for generating creativity. Most of these techniques play variations on two basic mental processes: making unusual or interesting connections between ideas, and reversing or challenging some aspect of the matter being considered. Combining, transforming or inverting mental elements: creativity as a set of techniques has a definite whiff of the alchemical about it.

One thing is clear. To innovate is, simply, to create something new. What, then, are we looking for when we are looking for creativity? A personality trait? A particular set of skills? A discipline mediated by a set of techniques?

'SOMETHING SPECIAL' – CREATIVITY AS A COMPETENCE

Perhaps you decide to see creativity as an inborn trait; an inherited predisposition that only some people possess, like being able to roll your tongue lengthwise. Given this assumption, generating and harnessing creativity means finding the most creative people. Creativity becomes a recruitment issue.

But what does a 'creative person' look like? How do you find them? How can you tell a creative type when recruiting? Might there be a set of competencies that would 'code for' creativity?

Cognitive psychologists and others have studied creativity in depth over the years; their work has developed into a school of creativity that seeks out essential elements of 'the creative personality'. We might regard the cognitive models they have created as competency maps that could serve as the foundation for job specifications.

CREATIVITY – THE 'SNOWFLAKE MODEL'

Based on a number of studies, a competency map for creativity might look something like this.

✓ **Displays a personal aesthetic.** Has the urge to make complexity simple. Seeks out patterns, associations and resemblances. Displays a high tolerance of ambiguity, asymmetry and uncertainty.

✓ **Displays a talent for seeking out problems.** Looks for the unanswered questions. Prefers the most awkward problem. Has an insatiable curiosity for the next challenge, the next conundrum. Loves research and hungers for more information.

✓ **Demonstrates mental mobility.** Can look at a situation in many different ways. Turns ideas inside out, back to front, upside down. Can pull a sequence of assumptions apart and ask 'What if?' Loves metaphors and analogies. Will explain or describe situations using unusual images or turns of phrase.

✓ **Is willing to take risks.** Likes to live dangerously. Seeks excitement and constant stimulation; easily bored. Is continually seeking out unknown territory to explore. Displays a healthy acceptance of failure. Likes to work at the edge of their competence; this may at times involve improvizing or even 'flying by the seat of their pants'.

✓ **Demonstrates objectivity about their own work.** Seeks out opinions about their work. Takes criticism and integrates it into their future work. Thrives on feedback.

✓ **Displays self-motivation.** Does it for the thing itself. Driven by a passion for the task itself, a passion to create. Little interest in reward, salary or perks. Unlikely to alter performance based on external forms of motivation – evaluation or assessment. Impatient of supervision.

Such a person specification might look like the blueprint for the ideal innovator. But how easy would such a person be to manage? Creative people, it is often said, are not easy to work with. A team member displaying any of the competencies in our job specification may become alienated in their own team. They can become a 'lone creative', misunderstood by other team members as self-serving, disruptive and a rule-breaker. Their manager must protect them while ensuring that team norms don't suffer: providing support, stimulating new ideas and protecting them in the early stages.

Team role analysis may help. Belbin's famous team role model, for example, includes the 'plant', a role that encompasses creativity and imagination. Identifying the 'plant' in a team may help to give them more credibility with other team members. Once known as the resident creative – the 'team jester' perhaps – they may be able to enjoy more freedom to ask awkward questions, to suggest unusual solutions and to pursue their own work in their own way. The challenge is to foster a culture in which 'plants' can work creatively without undermining the overall functions of the team.

CREATIVE AND RATIONAL THINKING – THE CONSTRUCTED DIVIDE

Another school of creativity sees it as a skill that can be learned. Maybe creativity is not a quality enjoyed only by a few gifted 'plants'; maybe it is a set of activities that anybody can develop. Such a view would certainly help to demystify it and make it more accessible. Looked at in this way, creativity usually takes on a new name: it becomes 'creative thinking'.

Creative thinking is often defined in opposition to 'normal' thinking. 'Normal' thinking is seen as logical, rational, analytical and critical; creative thinking is illogical, emotional, irrational, holistic and associative. 'Normal' thinking leads to a predetermined answer, constrained by the rules of the situation. It tends to preserve existing habits of thinking. Creative thinking, on the other hand, is thinking 'outside the box' – a remarkably persistent phrase and image to emerge when people discuss creativity. It is the thinking that challenges assumptions, breaking habits of thought, 'rewriting the script'. It's often thought of, too, as 'extraordinary'; both outside the normal boundaries of thought, and rare. Creative thinking is often allied with artistic talent and notions of genius, both of which are assumed to minority attributes in the general population.

This dualism is an old one. It goes back at least to distinctions in 19th century philosophy between the 'Apollonian' and 'Dionysiac': between logical, rational thought and hot-blooded, passionate genius. From Jekyll and Hyde to the Vulcan Spock, the dichotomy between cool rationality and creative passion has been a *leitmotif* in European and American culture throughout the last century. It's an idea firmly embedded in our social consciousness.

This model of two opposed types of thinking is attractive. It can usefully help us extend the boundaries of our thinking. Two points, however, deserve emphasis.

- First, creative thinking, like any thinking, works best when it is disciplined. It is not 'free-form' thinking in which anything goes. To be effective, it must be harnessed to a clear purpose and exercised according to clear rules of procedure.
- Secondly, it is only part of the journey towards innovation. Both kinds of thinking have their place: to value creativity at the expense of cool-headed reason is just as dangerous as ignoring creativity altogether. Managers may become more comfortable with creative thinking if they understand that it forms part of a larger strategy; a process that can be organized and managed.

THE TWO STAGES OF THINKING

We can imagine thinking as a process in two stages: perception and judgement.

1 In the first stage, we **perceive** reality and name what we have perceived. The end result of first-stage thinking is that we *encode* reality in language: words, numbers, diagrams, pictures, maps, etc.
2 In the second stage, we **judge** what we have perceived. Second-stage thinking manipulates language purposefully.

THE TWO STAGES OF THINKING

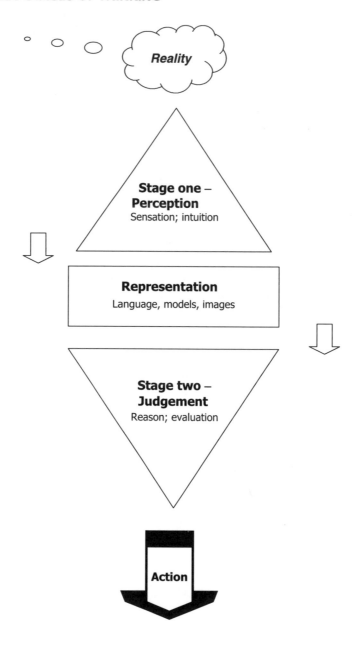

Perception determines what we know; judgement determines what we know about what we know – and what we might do about it.

Carl Jung, the great Swiss psychoanalyst, postulated four psychic functions, which we can add to this simple model.

We perceive using *sensation* (our five senses) and *intuition* (perception using the unconscious or our 'sixth' sense). We judge using *reason* (analysis, logic) and *feeling* or *evaluation* (using scales or codes of value to estimate the worth or value of something). Jung himself defined these four functions with great simplicity in his great popularizing book, *Man and his Symbols*.

> 'Sensation tells you that something exists; thinking tells you what it is; feeling tells you whether it is agreeable or not; and intuition tells you whence it comes and where it is going.'

(These four psychic functions are well known as the basis of the Myers-Briggs psychometric test.)

All thinking follows these two stages. Second-stage thinking is impossible without first-stage thinking. And the quality of our second-stage thinking depends directly on our ability to think well at the first stage. The way we perceive, and name, reality will determine how we judge it and then act on it.

However, we tend to be better at second-stage thinking than at first-stage thinking. We can even build machines to do it for us: computers manipulate language to achieve precise outcomes. In fact, we are so good at judging, choosing, solving and getting results that we tend to ignore first-stage thinking: we tend to take our perceptions for granted. We 'leap to judgement' or 'jump to conclusions'.

Creative thinking is most valuable at the first stage, where it can help us to develop and transform our perception. Our capacity to judge and evaluate ideas is already well trained. It is our ability to *generate* ideas that we need to develop.

INTUITION – THE UNSUNG DIMENSION OF FIRST-STAGE THINKING

The challenge in developing creative thinking is to find a way of systematizing intuition.

Intuition is the perception of possibilities inherent in a situation. Intuition can tell us how a situation may have arisen, how it may develop and what it might mean. Intuition can also suggest possible ways of responding to the situation.

The problem is that intuition – by definition – is unconscious. First-stage thinking uses both sensation and intuition. Improving the use of our five senses is relatively straightforward; we simply feed them more and different stimulation. Indeed, a good deal of creativity training and consultancy aims to excite the five senses through art, sport, music or theatre, or simply by taking people into a new and attractive environment. But gaining access to our power of intuition is not so easy.

Intuition, after all, is perception using the unconscious; how can we consciously regulate the way our unconscious operates?

THE FOUR STAGES OF INTUITIVE THINKING

Intuition became systematized as part of a model of the creative process in Graham Wallas' book *The Art of Thought,* published in 1926. Working in part from information he had received years before, Wallas formulated a four-stage model of the creative process.

1 **Preparation**, the first stage, involves working at a problem, investigating it and gathering information. This hard work is essential to prepare the unconscious mind for what is to follow.

2 **Incubation** is the second stage. The conscious mind 'lets go' of the problem and we 'sleep on it'; perhaps literally, perhaps metaphorically by engaging with some other activity. The material sinks into our unconscious, where intuition sets to work.

3 Illumination occurs when elements of the problem 'click' into a new pattern; what Wallas calls a 'happy idea'. The mind leaps to a new perception, radically altering our view of the problem.

4 Validation, finally, is the stage where we check our new insight against reality, applying logic and evaluation to judge its worth.

Wallas' model is important for a number of reasons.

- The model is recognizable; we have all had the moments of illumination that follow the incubation of an idea.
- It acknowledges that intuitive insight plays a part within the creative process. Intuition must have material to work on, and we must work consciously to feed it. Our intuitions must also succumb to rigorous critical validation if they are to contribute to worthwhile results.
- The model reinforces the importance of slow reflective thought in the creative process; intuition will not be hurried.
- Wallas suggests a method we might adopt to give intuition a chance in generating new ideas.

Intuition is the mental faculty that shifts mental patterns and disrupts mindsets. In dreams, jokes or hunches, our mental patterns become more fluid; we make unusual associations that suggest new ways of interpreting experience. Generally, such discontinuous changes in perception occur when the mind is at its most relaxed; while we are asleep, for example, or exercising. It is at such times that intuitive perceptions come to us unbidden. But work – especially innovative work – is a structured activity: simply waiting for intuition to strike is impractical. Somehow, we need techniques that will deliberately stimulate our intuition; techniques that offer more than just sporadic insights; techniques that managers and researchers might use systematically. The history of creativity since Wallas has largely been the story of attempts to create such techniques.

BRAINSTORMING – THE FATHER OF ALL CREATIVITY TECHNIQUES?

Alex Osborn invented brainstorming in the 1930s. Osborn was an advertising executive with an evangelical passion to liberate the latent creativity of ordinary people. Fired in particular by the demands of post-war reconstruction, he developed a simple process for idea generation. His formidable ability to sell his idea won brainstorming a large following throughout the 1950s and 1960s.

Brainstorming has not always had a smooth ride. Laboratory studies in the 1960s suggested that it might not be as effective as other methods of generating ideas. But even more damaging was an article in *Fortune* magazine in the late 1950s, which called brainstorming 'weird' and 'cerebral popcorn'. Industrial sponsorship for Osborn and his ideas dried up overnight and it was years before brainstorming regained its former popularity.

Alex Osborn himself set four simple rules for a successful brainstorming session.

ALEX OSBORN'S FOUR RULES OF BRAINSTORMING

1 **Criticism is ruled out.** Ideas are to be judged later, not during the session.

2 **'Freewheeling' is welcome.** The wilder the idea, the better. It's easier to tame down than to think up.

3 **We want more!** The more ideas, the greater the likelihood of a good one.

4 **Combine and improve.** As well as contributing ideas, team members should suggest ways of improving, combining or varying others' ideas.

Beyond this now-famous manifesto, Osborn emphasized four key principles.

- **Get going** – don't wait for inspiration to strike.
- **Focus** – on the objective of the session, what you want to achieve.
- **Pay attention** – make sure the whole team is thinking in only one way at a time.
- **Concentrate** – stick at it, refusing to give up if no ideas come.

Any brainstorming session needs to be well planned if it is to follow these principles. Osborn himself offered few more detailed techniques to help the session along.

ARTHUR KOESTLER AND THE IDEA OF BISOCIATION

Many thinkers have sought to stimulate intuition through associative thinking. Intuitive experiences can create new and unexpected associations in the mind, and it is these associations that are the 'creative sparks' of new ideas.

The most influential writer on this subject in recent decades has been Arthur Koestler. Koestler's *The Act of Creation*, published in 1964, was a landmark in popular writing on creativity. Koestler called his book an overview of 'the conscious and unconscious processes underlying artistic originality, scientific discovery and comic inspiration'. He explored what he termed 'bisociative thinking', the associations the mind creates by perceiving the same situation or idea 'in two self-consistent but habitually incompatible frames of reference'. The simplest example of a bisociation is a pun, in which the mind sees a word as having two meanings simultaneously.

The creative act, according to Koestler, activates the mind on more than one level. His study was partly a reaction to the then prevalent behaviourist view of humans as highly conditioned creatures. Koestler's emphasis on the power of associative thinking seemed to liberate mental life from the sterile Pavlovian realm of stimulus and response. He saw the mind as something transformative and creative. His hope was that, if the act of creation involves bisociative thinking, we might be able to stimulate creativity by deliberately fostering such bisociations. And the key to such deliberate efforts is metaphor.

EDWARD DE BONO AND LATERAL THINKING

Koestler's star has faded in the years since his death. His enormous influence in the 1960s has not, it seems, survived. Another figure, publishing his key ideas at about the same time as Koestler, has fared rather better in the popular imagination.

Edward de Bono first proposed the idea of 'lateral thinking' in the late 1960s. The phrase caught the public imagination and is now a part of everyday speech. De Bono plays a variation on the 'normal/creative' dichotomy and focuses on the thinking *processes* characterizing each.

De Bono distinguishes between what he calls 'vertical thinking' and 'lateral thinking'.

- **Vertical thinking** is traditional logical thinking. It proceeds step by step from problem to solution. Vertical thinking is concerned with finding the right answer; and you have to be right at each stage in order to get the right answer. Doing a sum is a classic example of vertical thinking.
- **Lateral thinking** jumps from one place to another. It is not concerned with finding the right answer but with finding a new idea. Consequently, being right at any stage is irrelevant in lateral thinking. The aim is not to solve but to find something new. Seeing how two seemingly dissimilar objects are alike is a classic example of lateral thinking.

Vertical thinking involves digging the same hole deeper; lateral thinking involves finding a more interesting or productive hole to dig.

De Bono's work is enormously influential and of genuine importance. He rescues creativity from the realm of the ineffable and unexplained, and offers realistic strategies for developing it as a practical strategy. Success, he insists, depends above all on focused *attention*. He calls many of his techniques 'Directed Attention Thinking Tools': one of the best known is the set of 'Six Thinking Hats', which direct the thinker's attention to only one kind of thinking at a time. If de Bono has a fault, it is that he tends to develop essentially simple ideas into structures of sometimes baffling complexity. Consequently, his ideas are probably more widely known about than practised.

OTHER CREATIVITY TECHNIQUES SINCE BRAINSTORMING

Many other creative thinking techniques have been developed in the decades since brainstorming was born. All more or less serve to stimulate associative thinking deliberately. They generally operate in three ways:

- by constructing sets of associations;
- through the use of metaphor; and
- by challenging or reversing the assumptions underlying our thinking.

CONSTRUCTIVIST CREATIVITY – TWO EXAMPLES

A number of techniques have grown up that seek to build on the 'more is better' philosophy of brainstorming. They work on the principle that large numbers of ideas, more or less mechanically generated, should provide at least the raw material for genuinely interesting new ideas.

MORPHOLOGICAL ANALYSIS

Morphological analysis simply means analysing by shape. As a creativity technique, it usually means creating a grid or matrix from three or more variables and studying the full set of combinations. The technique was apparently first developed in the 1940s by Fritz Zwicky, a Swiss astronomer working in astrophysics and rocket research. His name became well known in R&D circles during the 1960s, but his ideas – and the off-putting phrase 'morphological analysis' itself – tended to limit the range of his influence.

For example, an innovation team looking for new product opportunities might set up variables such as processes, markets and raw materials and plot them against each other in a grid or model. Certain combinations would stand out as existing products; other combinations might suggest new ideas: a potential or untried combination or process, raw material and market that might turn into a winning product.

This kind of analysis is often popular in industrial contexts, partly because it manages complex industrial situations with some clarity, and partly because it undoubtedly appeals to systematically minded technologists. It is not exactly 'creativity without the thinking', but it does give a rather mechanistic spin to creative thinking.

TRIZ

An extraordinary form of morphological analysis was developed in Russia during the 1940s and 1950s. With the collapse of Cold War politics, it is at last becoming more widely known.

Genrik Saulovich Altschuler was a Russian patent inspector who claimed to have discovered underlying patterns of invention through the systematic study of thousands of patents. He wrote to Stalin in 1948 criticizing the Soviet state's inability to stimulate invention, and was promptly sentenced to 25 years' imprisonment in Siberia. In the concentration camp, he continued to develop his ideas into a system: TRIZ (an acronym for a phrase meaning 'theory of inventive problem solving'). After Stalin's death in 1954, he was released and began to publish his ideas. However, he once again fell foul of the authorities in 1974, when TRIZ went underground and Altschuler was forced to support himself by writing science fiction. TRIZ only resurfaced with *perestroika* in the late 1980s. Since then, it has steadily gained a worldwide audience.

TRIZ is founded on the principle of dialectical materialism. Every system contains a struggle between opposites; the contradictions are resolved as the system develops. Seeking out new ideas is the systematic process of identifying the conflicting opposites in a situation and then finding a way of resolving them. It seems that the method has been systematized to the point where researchers can use a matrix or grid to locate the problem-solving technique to be used for any one of a multitude of paired opposites. Altschuler claims to have discovered the principles governing such dialectical development; they can be trained so that creativity becomes less hit-and-miss and more systematic.

CASE STUDY

LEARNING FROM THE PAST – OXFORD CREATIVITY AND TRIZ

One of the promoters of TRIZ in the UK is Oxford Creativity, a consultancy set up by Karen Gadd and Darrell Mann. Karen had previously founded Music at Oxford; Darrell is a former Rolls Royce engineer. Another engineer from Rolls, Henry Hornyold-Strickland, has now joined them.

Oxford Creativity runs short seminars, one- and two-day courses and longer events with client companies. Gadd is passionate about TRIZ. 'There are no technical problems that TRIZ is unable to solve,' she claims. 'That sounds extreme, but TRIZ offers conceptual solutions for all problems. Implementation difficulties then become new problems, and TRIZ can be used to resolve those problems as well.'

TRIZ seems to make its biggest mark in technical fields. 'The reason why companies like Rolls Royce are so interested in it is that it increases their ability to solve technical problems,' says Karen. 'TRIZ is very much about understanding that we can learn from the past; we don't have to tackle every new problem completely cold.'

TRIZ is gaining steadily in popularity. A thriving on-line journal (www.triz-journal.com) offers a wealth of material about the technique.

SYNECTICS AND THE POWER OF METAPHOR

Another set of creativity techniques grows out of brainstorming's rules about 'freewheeling' and combining ideas to create new ones. Finding wild ideas led some practitioners in the direction of metaphor. A number of techniques have sought to systematize metaphor-making; of these, perhaps the most famous is Synectics.

Synectics grew out of the work of two men: WJJ Gordon and George Prince. Gordon tape-recorded design engineers at work and discovered that the team entered an observably different psychological state prior to breakthrough discoveries. Cool, objective analysis gave way to a more metaphorical and engaged style that Gordon dubbed 'hot'. Might it be possible to induce this state in an innovation team deliberately?

Gordon introduced a number of procedures designed to increase the chances of stimulating the 'hot' style of thinking; among them, his use of metaphor was particularly powerful. Gordon continued to develop this side of the work; his former colleague, George Prince, developed a system of social dynamics that is designed to foster metaphorical thinking.

Synectics takes up where brainstorming leaves off. It develops Alex Osborn's ideas and generates a more systematic process where individual roles, process disciplines and interpersonal skills are carefully monitored. An important element in a Synectics session is an 'excursion' in which the team is led away from the 'goal as understood' – the innovation to be striven for – into a metaphorical landscape where the goal can be perceived in new and surprising ways. For example, the team leader might identify an example of some quality in the initial situation and ask the team for examples of the same quality in completely different contexts. A bridge might become a gesture of friendship; a car engine might turn into a community celebration, generating money rather than forward movement. The deliberately generated metaphor encourages associative thinking and intuitive insight.

Synectics remains one of the most systematic approaches to creative thinking developed. It has won considerable support in industrial and business settings and continues to give its name to a consultancy. However, its name is not as well known as it should be, partly because Gordon and Prince's own work is not easily available. Prince's book, *The*

Practice of Creativity, in particular, is hard to find. This is a pity, as it is a valuable summary of his ideas, both about the structured use of metaphor and the team dynamics necessary for Synectics to succeed.

ASSUMPTION CHALLENGE AND RULE REVERSAL

A number of creativity techniques seek to stimulate creativity by breaking mindsets. The aim of these techniques is to reveal and challenge the assumptions lying behind our thinking.

All thinking starts from assumptions. It is impossible to think without them. And every assumption we make rests on another, deeper assumption. Every assumption might be challenged to suggest new ideas. These techniques assume – for the purpose of stimulating new ideas – that every assumption, potentially, is up for grabs.

These techniques are usually the hardest to use well. By definition, assumptions tend to be unconscious; surfacing them can be difficult. We tend also to cling to our assumptions as values and beliefs; challenging them can involve discomfort, pain or even hostility. It is important to emphasize that challenges to these assumptions are first-stage thinking. They are not propositions to abandon long-held beliefs; they are imaginative excursions away from reality. The aim of the exercise is not to suggest real solutions but to provoke new thinking.

Assumption challenge follows a three-step process. First, we must identify an assumption that might be underlying our thinking. Once identified, we can challenge the assumption by asking 'What if..?' This question points towards a hypothetical situation in which the assumption doesn't apply: 'What if this assumption didn't hold?' We might take the question a step further and seek to *reverse* the assumption: 'What if the reverse of this assumption were true?'

In the new, imaginary world where the assumption has been flouted or overturned, we can explore the implications and imagine new kinds of solutions. These we might suggest as questions beginning 'How about..?'

Identify assumption	⇨	What if . . ?	⇨	How about . . ?

Identifying assumptions can be the trickiest part of the task. Various checklists can help to make the job easier. For example, assumptions in organizational settings include rules and concepts; these might be surfaced and challenged in a systematic way.

TWO TYPES OF ASSUMPTIONS

1 Rules
- Laws
- Procedures
- 'Unwritten rules'
- Habits
- Morals
- Regulations
- Quality standards
- Mottoes and slogans
- Conventions
- Cultural constraints (ethnic; gender; organizational)

2 Concepts
- Physical arrangements
- Definitions
- Job descriptions
- Priorities
- Customers
- Field of operation
- Methods
- Strategy
- Timetable
- The business we're in

ROBERT FRITZ AND CREATING

One practitioner stands apart from all this work on creative thinking techniques. Robert Fritz is a composer and consultant who has developed a distinctly different approach to creativity. Indeed, he dislikes the very word, preferring to talk about *creating*. In his books, *The Path of Least Resistance* and *Creating: a guide to the creative process*, Fritz outlines his views on what makes us creative and how we can be more successful in creating. Fritz is an important figure, if only because of his association with Peter Senge (author of *The Fifth Discipline*) and his increasingly public presence in the business arena. In 1996, he published his views on organizational change, *Corporate Tides*.

Fritz is openly scornful of most creativity techniques. 'Can you imagine,' he writes, 'Mozart brainstorming alternatives for the overture to *The Marriage of Figaro*?' For Fritz, these techniques leave out the vital question of the creative process: 'What do I want to create?' His concern is with the process that brings something new and valuable into existence. That process is born out of a vision of the creation desired, and continues by developing the craft of creating.

Fritz's insistence that creativity only makes sense in the context of a *desire to create something* is a powerful reminder that generating ideas is only useful as part of a larger, creative purpose.

Fritz notes that creativity and problem solving are often mentioned in the same breath. Creating and solving problems, he insists, are different activities. Problem solving is taking action to make something go away; creating is taking action to bring something into being. Problem solving arises from what Fritz calls a 'reactive-responsive orientation', in which our action is based on the circumstances in which we find ourselves. Reacting and responding to circumstances becomes a circular system in which real creativity is impossible. To start creating, we have to shift into the 'creative orientation'. In this orientation, we are not the victims of circumstances but use these circumstances as one of the forces in the creative process.

The creative orientation is dominated by the desire to create. It is not a matter of 'liberating creativity', of 'taking risks' or 'manufacturing commitment'; these are all responses to the perceived lack of creativity, risk or commitment and so sit within the reactive mode. Creating is bringing something into being for its own sake.

FIVE STEPS TO CREATING

Fritz suggests that the creating process follows five identifiable steps.

1 **Conceive.** Have an idea of what you want to create. It may be general or specific. Before you can start to create, you must know what you want to bring into being.

2 **Know what currently exists.** This may be surprisingly hard to do. We tend to view reality with various biases – assumptions, values, beliefs – that distort the truth of what actually exists. But unless you know what currently exists in relation to your ambition, you cannot take action towards creating it.

3 **Take action.** What do you do? Fritz suggests some deceptively simple answers. 'Make it up.' 'Trial and error.' His point is that you do whatever you think is necessary to bring the creation nearer to existence. Some of the actions you take will move directly towards the desired result; most will not. 'The art of creating is often found in your ability to adjust or correct what you have done so far.' The 'right first time' philosophy is extremely unhelpful when trying to create something new. Creating involves learning as you go; and that, suggests Fritz, is a skill to be practised and learnt.

4 **Learn the rhythms of the creative process.** These are: germination, assimilation, completion. Germination begins with the excitement of the new; assimilation is living with your ideas and actions and helping them to pull together; completion is the final stage when you can see the end result and are re-energized to push for its full realization.

5 **Create momentum.** The creative process contains the seeds of its own development. Produce one creation and you will be better prepared to create the next.

This simple model might be the pattern of an innovation project. Fritz offers insights into the states of mind and activities that can help individuals and teams to create. He identifies the pitfalls and tensions that might arise along the way. Above all, he emphasizes that creating must be purposeful.

WHY BE CREATIVE?

Fritz touches on an important question facing innovators. What do we want to create? Creativity is not self-evidently desirable. It is only useful in support of the creative process. That process must be focused on goals and results just as much as any other organizational activity. But the goals of creating are not those of operational functioning. The goal of creating is to bring something new into existence. We shall not innovate while locked into the 'reactive-responsive' orientation that characterizes most of our work. We must use different competencies and skills, different thinking techniques and different work structures.

Fritz also points up an interesting paradox. Creating must be purposeful, yet it is its own justification. We create out of a desire to see the creation brought into existence. External motivation – return on investment, breaking even, reward, praise from others – are of little importance. In the 'creative orientation' we act out of a desire to bring the new into being. This paradox returns us to some of the enduring problems surrounding the management of innovation. Linking it to wider strategies, for example, may remove some of the energy that drives people to innovate. Evaluating or rewarding innovation may actually demotivate. On the other hand, clear objectives will certainly help to bring people into a creative orientation. To quote Fritz himself:

'There is nothing wrong with wanting better processes or studying the methods others have used. But too often people forget the fundamental purpose of any process – the result it serves.'

3

Establishing a culture of innovation

Innovation doesn't happen everywhere, all of the time. Creativity is the wellspring of innovation, but successful innovation requires more; certain conditions – social, economic and political – seem to be necessary. Innovation needs a culture in which to thrive; a rich mix of expertise and experience that opens windows in the cathedrals of our minds, leading to new ideas, new processes and new products. Some interesting questions come to mind: What might such conditions be? Could we recreate them deliberately?

'Culture' is a word we use both for societies and for organizations. It is a word almost as difficult to define as 'innovation', but in this context we are referring to the complex of values and attitudes that informs what people do. These values can be hard to discern: most of them are implicit rather than articulated in laws or other documents.

Some cultures seem to be more conducive to innovation than others. What are the values of such cultures? If we could identify them, perhaps we could foster them deliberately. This ambition has driven the development of industrial complexes, science parks and change programmes within organizations.

In this chapter, we examine how the values of cultures conducive to innovation might work – at the level of a whole society, as drivers of innovative activity in networks of organizations, and within organizations themselves.

MAKING LOVE IN A STRAITJACKET – THE BRITISH APPROACH TO CREATIVITY

The British may have a good reputation for creativity, but turning those ideas into reality (innovations) has proved more problematic. Simon Sholl, a Brit himself, is a man with a mission; he wants to change the way the British innovate. The task, he warns, will not be easy; for Sholl, it demands nothing less than a radical reorientation of the way people do business.

Sholl starts with a striking image. 'Not many people,' he says, 'would choose to make love in a straitjacket. It would be cumbersome, uncomfortable and not much fun – but, above all, the failure rate would be unacceptably high. Yet I believe that much of British management and marketing is doing the equivalent, in an environment where innovation suffers the "death of a thousand cuts" and creativity is regarded with suspicion or outright derision.'

As Planning and Development Director at Siebert Head, the international packaging, design and identity consultants, Sholl should know what he's talking about. He is in marketing and brand development; usually considered the most creative of businesses. Yet his heart regularly sinks when he has to enter into a long-term relationship with a UK client. He began to wonder: What is it about British organizations in particular that hampers creativity and stops them innovating as well as they might?

Towards the end of 1999, the German consultancy Agamus Consult produced *Stars of Innovation*, a report on levels of innovation in the principal 13 Western industrialized countries. How did Britain do? 'Well,' answers Sholl, 'we weren't at the bottom in terms of actual innovation, but neither were we at the top. Britain came sixth in terms of actual innovation, behind the US, Canada, Switzerland, Germany and Japan. However, we were *perceived* by the other twelve countries as being ninth.'

Is this just a PR problem? 'The story is actually a little more complicated,' says Sholl. In-depth interviews showed that, in terms of the amount of pressure the British put themselves under to innovate, they were right at the bottom of the table in 12th place. The British aren't, apparently, very good at motivating themselves to be creative. They don't have a creative culture that makes innovation natural and intuitive. Yet their innovation projects are the second most labour-intensive. They use more employees, less effectively, than just about anyone else – and yet they don't think that innovation is very important. Why?

First, class. Secondly, education.

Sholl is scathing about the way class relationships persist in British society. 'Our national psyche has inherited a pre-Industrial Revolution distinction between "Gentlemen" and "Trade". In my own field, this prejudice affects our relationships both with our clients and our colleagues. In our clients, it gives rise to a "supplier mentality". Class and education breed an innate fear of ideas in those who lead. This fear translates into a general distrust among clients of experts – and therefore of consultants, whom the clients hire for their expertise. I see it in my own business. Client and consultant all too often operate an "I pay the bills, you do as I say" relationship. This is not unlike hiring a heart surgeon to operate on you and then proceeding to instruct them in where to make the first incision. As a result, our clients may get what they want, but they rarely get what they need. In such circumstances, innovation – genuine, cross-disciplinary innovation; the only sort that works – is well nigh impossible. The situation is starkly different in relatively classless societies such as Scandinavia or Germany, where most clients respect and act on the advice and expertise of the consultants they have hired.'

Sholl suggests that this supplier mentality affects not just client relationships, but the internal structures of organizations. 'Advertising agencies, creative consultancies and packaging designers, for example – the kinds of organizations I know best – are organized according to principles, beliefs and systems that grew up in the 19th century. "Gentlemen" in suits still write copy and represent the agency, while "the inky chaps in the studio" do the illustrations. Creativity is regarded as Trade, very much in the same way that a gentleman farmer would have regarded a blacksmith in 1899. The "Suit" takes the brief from the client and instructs the "Creatives" what to do. In due course, the Creatives show what they have done to the Suits, and the results are presented to the client.

Creatives who dispute the brief are "stroppy". Suits who don't like the work "don't understand creativity". The two tribes remain at loggerheads. In the meantime, creativity, like desire in the straitjacket, quietly withers away.'

Sholl sees the class system reflected in our education system 'or, more exactly, systems, because in Britain we have two.' Most leaders and opinion-formers in the UK were educated either in public schools or in schools modelled on the public school system. 'This style of education,' says Sholl, 'is based on the "learn, don't question" principle. The other education system is based on the principle that the answer's not as important as the process. If imagination isn't important in the old system, it sometimes seems that education isn't important in the "new" system. Either way, I think we're missing something. People who succeed through creativity seem to me to have done so, more often than not, in spite of their education rather than because of it.'

This marginalizing of the creative is no doubt visible in many organizations in many different cultures: the inability to manage fragile new ideas, the exercise of power to stifle initiative, the wielding of knowledge to trash subordinates. But Sholl sees it as a peculiarly British problem. 'A number of things add up: our class assumptions, our anti-commercialism and the "memes" (governing ideas) that are fed into us by our education.'

What, then, needs to change? What are the key drivers in education, government and industry that will liberate the British from the straitjacket and encourage real innovation?

First, education. Sholl values the Socratic model of learning.

'This model is based on dialogue – a rich conversation between teacher and pupil. It doesn't devalue the teacher's expertise; but it does assume that teacher and pupil are on some fundamental level equals. By putting forward ideas, by discussing and exploring them, both teacher and pupil share in learning – in opening their minds. The Socratic method of learning requires self-discipline and a deep respect, for both teacher and pupil. We need to develop an educational system that encourages a fascination with ideas and a willingness to open our minds to them. We need, too, to develop in our education a respect for commerce. Commerce contributes to a better way of life and creates the wealth that, apart from anything else, pays for education.'

What of government?

'We need to destroy the political cadre that results in governmental isolation,' asserts Sholl, 'and perhaps also the professional cadre that seems to assume that a background in the Inns of Court automatically qualifies you to run the country. Maybe we should end career politics.'

And industrial practice? How can the British encourage innovation in their organizations, in their great corporations and myriad consultancies? 'Well, we certainly need to move beyond the suggestion box. A good ideas scheme should revolve around Socratic dialogue, where you can bring an idea to somebody who will discuss it with you, working out where the nugget of genius lies.'

Sholl's ideas come thick and fast. 'We need to create a culture of daring. We should institutionalize the office party, so that the freedom to say what we really think extends beyond the once-a-year binge. We should kill off the brainstorm. Or rather, brainstorms need to be managed properly. We should allow people their personal ambitions. We should use research as a creative tool.'

But in the end, he returns to class. 'To force a switch from the reactive to the innovative means creating new management and reporting systems that put an end to the reiterative, approval-seeking approach to decision making. It means breaking down functional barriers and the tribal cultures that go with them. It means an enforced meritocracy (and maybe an end to job titles and individual offices). Above all, it means recognition, at an organizational level, that innovation is not the prerequisite of any one department.'

It seems a lot to ask. 'Like making love in a straitjacket? Well, yes. But I do seriously think that innovation and making love have some similarities. Both are creative. Both require technique and instinct. In the end, of course, innovation is about creating new, saleable products and services. It's the way we manage technique and instinct *together* that creates saleable products.'

Sholl smiles and shrugs. 'Who knows? The British may shake off that straitjacket yet.'

CHAOS AND CREATIVITY – THE INDUSTRIAL DISTRICT AS A CULTURE OF INNOVATION

Innovation is overwhelmingly an urban phenomenon. Historically, creativity has tended to arise, not in remote rural areas, but in densely populated cities. In fact, innovation seems to happen in particular cities at particular times. And any one city seems to enjoy its moment of glory only once.

Over a century ago, the economist Alfred Marshall noticed that innovation flourished in certain types of areas. He found such areas, for example, in London's East End, in Manchester, Stoke-on-Trent, Birmingham and Glasgow. He called them 'industrial districts' and explained how they fostered innovation.

> 'When an industry has chosen a locality for itself, it is likely to stay there long: so great are the advantages which people following the same skilled trade get from near neighbourhood to one another. The mysteries of the trade become no mysteries; but are as it were in the air, and children learn many of them unconsciously. Good work is rightly appreciated, inventions and improvements in machinery, in processes and the general organization of the business have their merits promptly discussed: if one man starts a new idea, it is taken up by others and combined with suggestions of their own; and thus it becomes the source of further new ideas.'

This passage – with its striking description of what we would today call 'brainstorming' – brings the idea of an innovative culture to life. It could just as well describe the clusters of hi-tech companies working in Silicon Valley or the 'virtual' networks of software houses, design companies, microelectronics manufacturers and assemblers, and service providers developing in the 'dot.com' arena.

Such districts display some of the characteristics of complexity theory. For example, production is 'vertically disintegrated': a large number of individually owned enterprises produces the materials or components for each other, creating production networks of great complexity. Companies must cluster together to ease the problems of transport and compatibility. But such economic complexity, crucially, also creates the social complexity of *communities*, in which people meet, learn from each other and exchange ideas. The meeting of minds is as crucial to the growth of innovation as the production networks.

Economists and geographers since Marshall have sought the key features of such innovative milieux. Peter Hall, for example, in his extensive book *Cities in Civilization*, studies Manchester in the 18th century, Glasgow and Berlin in the 19th, Detroit at the turn of the 20th and San

Francisco in the mid-20th century. He sees a number of features shared by all of these great industrial areas.

- They are **trading centres**. Many are ports.
- They **grow and decline around innovative activity.** Technological innovation *generates* urban development. These cities grow fast – often explosively. And their decline, as innovation moves elsewhere, can be catastrophic.
- These cities are **at the edge of economic and cultural areas.** They are located mid-way between established centres of industrial and political power. They are not isolated, but they are definitely marginal.
- They have a **tradition of development in related industrial fields.** The successful enterprises satisfy a demand internal to the local market: ships in Glasgow, Model T Fords for local farmers in Detroit, electronics for the military in San Francisco. Often, innovation arises from a dialogue between related, established industries.
- They enjoy **relative cultural freedom** – from stifling prejudice, from tradition, from political or social restraint. They enjoy egalitarian social structures, with little inherited wealth. The religious or spiritual atmosphere, too, tends to encourage open thinking and achievement: Protestantism, Shintoism, Hedonism in the case of California!
- There is a **network of activity** that fosters learning and the exchange of ideas. Education is more or less freely available, either academically or – crucially – through apprenticeships. Channels exist to transfer knowledge to new applications.
- They benefit from **new wealth**, controlled by people who are willing to risk it in new ventures.

Two Swedish scholars have developed more theoretical models of an innovative culture. In 1978, Gunnar Törnqvist suggested that any innovative culture contains four key elements:

- **information** transmitted between people;
- **knowledge** stored in real or mechanical memories;

- **competence** in activities relevant to the needs of an external environment;
- **creativity**, making something new out of these three activities.

Another Swedish scholar, Åke Andersson, has developed a similar concept. Andersson believes that a number of factors come together in 'a process of dynamic synergy' to create cultures of innovation:

- a sound, lightly regulated financial system;
- basic original knowledge and competence;
- an imbalance between experienced need and actual opportunities;
- a culturally diverse community;
- good communications.

Both Törnqvist and Andersson emphasize the idea of 'structural instability' in their models. This idea, too, has echoes of complexity theory. A culture becomes innovative, according to these models, 'at the edge of chaos': when its internal order is on the point of transition or radical transformation. Stable cultures – or cultures in a state of total collapse – tend to be seriously lacking in innovation. (Those of us working in well established, well ordered organizations – or decrepit, disorderly ones – may recognize the point all too well.) Interestingly, both Törnqvist and Andersson choose to explain this somewhat alarming concept of structural instability using the metaphor of a river; perhaps because Sweden is famous for its mighty rivers.

Imagine a culture pursuing its course through a social and economic 'landscape'. In the early stages of a culture's development, regulation and technology work together to produce a course that is fast-flowing and well defined. Later, the 'landscape' flattens. The culture may stagnate; alternatively, its course may become unclear and unstable. Uncertainty about the future provides the opportunity for creative change. A small group of visionaries can intervene and take the society into a new stable phase. These are Schumpeter's 'New Men', bold entrepreneurs who can adapt to the conditions of uncertainty.

TOP-DOWN OR BOTTOM-UP? TWO CULTURES OF INNOVATION

So far, we have seen innovation as essentially a 'bottom-up' phenomenon. Maverick individuals – visionary, subversive, on the margins of the established social order, often young – create chaotic networks of enterprises in which new ideas spark into life and innovation takes off energetically and unpredictably.

Two historical developments, however, complicate this account. They suggest that innovation also has a 'top-down' dimension; that, over the past century, it has been systematized and institutionalized within large corporations. For many of us, these developments have come to define how we experience innovation.

The first key development is the rise of research and development (R&D). During the late 19th century, in Germany and the US especially, industry – and the science that supports it – becomes institutionalized. The vertically disintegrated 'industrial district' becomes the highly integrated global corporation, controlling every aspect of production and distribution. The entrepreneur gives way to the manager. And innovation becomes the province not of the visionary individualist but of the research scientist working in a commercially funded laboratory. The first R&D lab was set up by Siemens in Germany in 1872. Later examples include the Bell laboratories and DuPont's developmental department, established in the 1920s. In telecommunications, pharmaceuticals and even automobiles, R&D has become the home of innovation in the world's largest corporations. As a result, it has become common practice to see innovation as belonging in only one part of the organization; the most important challenge in many large corporations is to drag innovation out of the lab and into the organization as a whole.

The second major development in innovation over the last century has been the growing involvement of the state. Once again, the birthplace is Germany. Berlin in the 19th century grew from an insignificant capital of a minor German state to become the powerhouse of the Prussian war machine. Innovation – and the educational institutions that supported it – was encouraged by the state for openly militaristic objectives. The later development of Silicon Valley in the 1940s and 1950s was also driven, at least in part, by military imperatives: in this case, the politics of the Cold War. Companies were funded massively by Washington to invest in R&D, and innovation became focused on increasingly sophisticated military technology.

The difference is in the way the industries are organized. In Berlin, two huge companies dominated industrial innovation: Siemens and AEG. In California, by contrast, Stanford University formed the growth point of a host of small firms. The growth of defence contracting spawned huge numbers of small, spin-off companies, financed by venture capital, to create a local self-replicating production complex. Stanford became home to a Research Institute but also to the world's first science park. Silicon Valley very quickly became an industrial district not unlike those of Victorian England. The network was held together initially by large contracts from big companies within the military-industrial complex; but it came also to depend on a highly localized pool of skills, knowledge and labour. It was this dynamic network of small enterprises – interdependent, highly competitive and yet highly collaborative – that helped to transform aeroplane manufacture into the new industry of aeronautics, and electronics into computer technology.

The influence of the state has also been a key factor in the other great innovative culture of the last century: Japan. The extraordinary success of Japanese corporations is an oft-told and complex story. A key player in that story is MITI: the Ministry of International Trade and Industry. Established in the 1920s, the ministry has its roots in the earliest years of the Meiji restoration, as early as the 1870s. Using a subtle system of tight social networks linking government, banking and industry, MITI established a system of consensus planning that guided the great Japanese corporations through the so-called 'catch up' period from 1950 to the mid-1970s. The role of government in Japan, however, is fundamentally different from the role of administrations in the US. During a period when military spending in Japan was severely limited, innovation became market-driven. Technological evolution has been at the service of what consumers will buy, rather than military ambitions at any cost. The great success of Japanese innovation has not been in creating fundamental new technologies, but in producing a flood of superbly produced consumer products, from cars to laptop computers. And this Japanese post-war miracle – whether it is now coming to an end or not – is built, in large part, on an intimate involvement by the state in companies' policy, strategy and funding.

THE SCIENCE PARK – VISION OF A NEW CULTURE OF INNOVATION?

Stanford's science park spawned a host of imitators around the world. Science parks are attempts to recreate deliberately the 'industrial districts' of the 19th century. The aim is to provide some equivalent of the older, chaotic culture of innovation, without the hideous social and environmental costs. Science parks marry the two traditions of innovation: the 'bottom-up' tradition of the small entrepreneurial enterprise founded in a garage or back bedroom, and the 'top-down' tradition of institutionalized innovation, organized within the research labs of large corporations and often supported or sponsored by the state.

The UK Science Park Association defines a science park as 'a business support and technology transfer initiative' that:

- encourages and supports the start up, incubation and development of innovation-led, high growth, knowledge-based businesses;
- provides an environment where larger and international businesses can develop specific and close interactions with a particular centre of knowledge creation for their mutual benefit; and
- has formal and operational links with centres of knowledge creation such as universities and research organizations.

A science park usually starts with some form of collaboration between government and higher education. One of the first science parks to be developed in the UK was in Cambridge. The project displays all the key characteristics of science parks: links between a large university (with, crucially, access to a large parcel of land), government and industry. The Labour government elected in 1964 had urged UK universities to increase their contact with industry, to increase the payback from investment in basic research. The Moot Committee, set up by the University of Cambridge, responded with a report in 1969. The committee recommended an expansion of 'science-based industry' close to Cambridge, to exploit the university's concentration of scientific expertise, equipment and libraries, and to increase feedback from industry into the Cambridge scientific community.

Trinity College, Cambridge, was impressed with these ideas. Trinity has a long tradition of scientific research and innovation, from Isaac Newton onwards. It also had a piece of land available. Located on the edge of Cambridge, it had belonged to the college since its foundation by King Henry VIII in 1546. It was farmland until World War II, when it was requisitioned by the US Army and used to prepare vehicles and tanks for the D-Day landings in Europe. After the war, the site lay largely derelict and increasingly threatened by planning blight until the decision to develop it.

Outline planning permission was granted in October 1971 and the first company, Laser-Scan, moved onto the site in 1973.

The park grew only slowly in the first five years. UK subsidiaries of multinational companies started to locate there (LKB Biochrom from Sweden and US laser specialists Coherent were the first) and the number of companies slowly grew to 25 by the end of the 1970s. The science park concept was an unfamiliar one; companies were initially attracted by the prospect of contact with university-based research. Trinity's willingness to weather slow returns on investment has played a big part in the park's later success. During the recessions of the 1980s and 1990s, the college remained committed to the concept of the park as a specialized location for hi-tech industry and research, and resisted the temptation to fill space with companies from other sectors.

The park began to take off in the 1980s. More starter units, and the Cambridge Innovation Centre, were built to expand the range of accommodation available. The Trinity Centre opened in 1984 to provide a meeting place, and a squash court was opened in 1986. The park now boasts a state-of-the-art conference centre and restaurants, a fitness centre and a nursery for 115 children.

The opening of a regional office for 3i marked the arrival of venture capital on the park. Spin-offs from existing tenant companies began to appear. The park's first collaborative venture was Qudos, founded by the university's microelectronics laboratory (by then located at the park), Prelude Technology Investments and Cambridge Consultants.

The life sciences sector has become the dominant technology sector in the park. A new biotech venture capital fund, Merlin Ventures, has recently opened an office there. There are now fewer but larger, better funded and more successful companies at the park and more of them are being launched onto the UK Stock Exchange. However, the origins of recent arrivals are much as they have always been: a mixture of spin-offs, developing new ventures from the Cambridge area and elsewhere in the UK, and UK subsidiaries of multinational companies. By 2000, 64 companies at the park were employing some 4,000 people.

CASE STUDY

GENERICS – MAKING THE RIGHT CONNECTIONS

If you can't find an industrial district, create your own. A mill on the outskirts of Cambridge houses one of Britain's most successful attempts to do just that.

Generics describes itself as 'a leading integrated technology consulting, development and investment organization'. Founded by Gordon Edge in 1986, the company's unique strength is its ability to create a synergy between three core activities: mixing powerful minds from different disciplines; consulting with some of the world's largest companies and turning business ideas into new companies in which Generics itself takes a stake. The company has strong roots in Cambridge but also has satellite operations in the US, Switzerland and, in particular, Sweden. The company floated on the London Stock Exchange in 2000.

Gordon Edge has not created this one-company culture of innovation overnight. His methods derive from a long career in consulting. Edge believes that innovation starts by creating the right conditions for interdisciplinary working. Generics' HQ contains offices and labs for over 200 employees working in biotechnology, telecommunications, microchip technology and optics. But the really new ideas emerge when researchers are exposed to the commercial needs of Generics' clients. The company encourages them to develop these ideas and has all the resources to help them start up or spin out into new enterprises. Generics then makes its own profit either through licensing or by selling its stake in a new business to an outsider.

New companies that have evolved in this way now employ hundreds of people, many of them still in the Cambridge area. Absolute Sensors, for example, makes new types of sensing equipment; Imerge supplies technology for televisions; Diomed makes surgical lasers.

Generics can support these new enterprises through the sensitive period when people go out on their own. A new company can even stay on the premises if it wishes.

Perhaps the most impressive aspect of Generics' achievement is the wide range of its activities. Three examples from the last 12 months illustrate the company's ability to work in an astonishing range of areas.

- Adaptive Screening Ltd (ASL) is a joint venture between Generics, the University of Glasgow and Imperial College of Science, Medicine and Technology. ASL aims to address the challenges of drug discovery in the post-genomic era by providing a new approach to pharmaceutical compound screening.
- Generics is working with Amey Datel to improve the quality of customer information on Britain's rail network.
- Generics has been working with Aqualisa on a revolutionary new shower, Quartz, which they successfully launched at the 'Bathroom

and Kitchen Show 2001' in London. Quartz's unique processor can be installed with ease in a remote location, leaving the bathroom wall free from unnecessary pipework and units. The one-touch shower controls are simple to operate, making it ideal for children and the elderly, and a light indicates when the temperature is safe to step into the shower.

Generics also supplies the network of contacts that helps its clients and spin-off companies to work more effectively. Gordon Baxter, a scientist who has been involved in two start-ups supported by Generics, explains: 'Through my Generics contacts I've been able to get in touch with people who can solve my problems and who would otherwise have been difficult to talk to.' It is this ability to create networks, within its own staff, between companies, and across the boundaries between commerce and academia, that makes Generics stand out as a shining example in a country where generating wealth from ideas has not always been successful. It is no surprise that, in February 2001, the company won the Visionary Leadership category in the 'Vision 100' competition organized by BT and Cranfield School of Management.

Cambridge's science park – with its attendant sites around the city, and now Microsoft's commitment to developing a new site to the west of the city – is a highly successful attempt to recreate deliberately the industrial district that Marshall had so vividly described in the late 19th century. The park contains everything necessary for the alchemy of innovative collaboration:

- a university with extensive resources and a world-class reputation for research;
- well developed consultancy, both technical and managerial;
- risk capital;
- sophisticated property management overseen by a landowner with a vested interest in intellectual and technological innovation; and

● a range of enterprises of different types in close proximity;

– all supported by the facilities and welcoming environment that make for the growth of a real community.

INTERNALIZING THE INDUSTRIAL DISTRICT – CREATING AN INNOVATIVE CULTURE INSIDE ORGANIZATIONS

So far, we have investigated the culture of innovation as it might operate within a society – either as an overarching influence or, more specifically, as the driver of innovative activity in networks of enterprises within an industrial district or its modern equivalents such as science parks. But can any of these ideas apply *within* organizations themselves? How might we begin to transform the cultures of our organizations so that they foster innovation more effectively?

It is a truism that most companies in the West are stiflingly uncreative. The only way to innovate, it seems, is to break out of 'the system' as a maverick entrepreneur. I think that this idea reflects a wider phenomenon in Western society: the cult of the individual. We value the individual as the source of creativity; we value organizations as emblems of social order; and we tend to see the two as being in opposition. As a result, we expect radical change to come about only through the efforts of heroic individuals, like the 'New Men' proclaimed by Joseph Schumpeter, either leading an organization charismatically or going it alone. 'If you want to get anything done,' we tell ourselves, 'do it yourself'. Place the individual inside an organizational structure and almost inevitably their creativity and initiative will wither.

This sense of tension between creative individualism and corporate inertia is not universally shared. In Japan, for example, corporations have been staggeringly successful in innovating, despite displaying many organizational characteristics that, in the West, might guarantee failure. Many of the most innovative Japanese corporations in the last five decades have been the biggest and the oldest – operating in a society that is well known for its essential conservatism. Over the years, writers have looked to Japan for lessons from which Western corporations might learn. Yet circumstances in post-war Japan have been substantially different from those of the US or a developed European economy; and the deeper features of Japanese culture are by no means easy to translate into a non-Japanese environment.

First, Japanese firms in the post-war period have had no choice but to innovate. Faced with several local wars in their region, intense international competition, numerous economic crises and increasingly volatile markets, Japanese companies have had to innovate simply to survive. Coping with uncertainty has been a matter of life or death even for the most successful Japanese companies. Western companies, by and large, have simply not faced such a life-and-death struggle to survive.

Secondly, Japanese culture places a strong emphasis on learning by doing. Since the establishment of Zen Buddhism, the Japanese have understood the oneness of body and mind. As a result, Japanese managers place a high value on experience as a teacher: they actively pursue new experiences and reflect at length on those experiences. In the West, by contrast, learning is regarded essentially as an academic activity. Learning gained through practical experience is systematically accorded less status than the learning gained in educational institutions – or from books.

Thirdly, Japanese society values the collective over the individual. Japanese firms are happy to exploit the knowledge of outside partners – suppliers, customers, outside specialists, even rival firms. They are past masters at internalizing such knowledge, reforming and enriching it to fit with their own company's identity and strategy. This sense of collective responsibility famously extends to the relationships between individuals and companies in Japan. Innovation in Japan relies strongly on the personal commitment of the employees and their identity with the company and its mission. Western organizations famously find it almost impossible to generate similar levels of loyalty or commitment in their workforces.

All three of these factors are hard to replicate in the West. We have not experienced the same desperate need to innovate; we tend systematically to downgrade the value of practical experience, preferring to award prestige and power to those with academic qualifications; and we live in a society that values individual achievement far above loyalty to any collective.

These, then, are the questions facing organizations in our part of the global village.

- How do we foster the sense of urgency that drives innovation?
- How do we balance an overly rational view of learning with a greater emphasis on experience and experiment?
- And how can we create a culture of commitment among workers who are likely to be highly individualistic in outlook?

SITES OF SPECIAL CREATIVITY – DEVELOPING INNOVATIVE ENVIRONMENTS

For many, the answer lies in improving the physical working environment. Managers are beginning to realize that silos are not conducive to creativity; that innovation work, in particular, is multi-disciplinary and will only flourish if people from different specialisms talk to each other. Hot-desking, cybercafés, new-start incubators and fit-out studios are all responses to this need to break down barriers and get people communicating. Some organizations have deliberately removed all communal areas from individual departments, so that people must move out of their immediate work areas to eat and drink. To go to the canteen or the coffee machine then entails mixing with people from other departments or disciplines.

CASE STUDY

STRETCHING THE WALLS – MULTI-DISCIPLINARY WORKING AT GLAXOSMITHKLINE

GlaxoSmithKline encourages multi-disciplinary teamwork at its New Frontiers Science Park in the UK. Everybody – from medicinal scientists to vascular biologists – is housed under one roof. 'What you tend to find with many companies,' explains Graham Holland, Director of Science Communications, 'is that you get particular sites or buildings that specialize in a certain discipline. But nothing in science is done in

> isolation. There's no point in keeping chemists in one building and biologists in another, when they really have to talk to each other on a daily basis and work in teams.'
>
> The working environment must also be flexible. Rapid response areas are built into the workplace. 'These are basically empty spaces,' says Holland. 'But they're a tacit acknowledgement that you don't know what the future will bring.' These spaces might quickly fill with new technology or research teams without the need to extend the building or move people off-site.

For others, an organization's culture is expressed, not only in its physical environment, but also in its managerial relationships. What kinds of organizational structures are most conducive to creating a culture of innovation?

We might imagine three broad types of organization: the 'top-down' model; the 'bottom-up' model; and the 'middle-management' model.

A 'top-down' organization is essentially an enterprise built in its owner's image. It is run by a charismatic individual with a vision of innovation. The leader inspires people in their organization by example. The freedom to innovate is born, somewhat paradoxically, out of a very personal vision that is imposed on the organization. Many innovative companies conform to this model; and many departments within larger organizations can be transformed, as if by magic, through the efforts of a single, inspirational leader. Such a model can be highly successful, but usually on a limited scale. The effects of inspirational leadership tend to dissipate as an enterprise grows in size – or when the leader leaves.

The 'bottom-up' model envisages a company or organization as a collection of smaller enterprises. A conglomerate might be made up of a large number of companies, each working to innovate in their own way and supported or sheltered from risk by the umbrella of the parent company. The classic example of such an organizational structure is 3M.

Nonaka and Takeuchi, in their ground-breaking book *The Knowledge-*

creating Company, suggest that middle management may have a crucial role to play in fostering innovation in more conventional companies. They recognize that middle management is conventionally viewed as the most resistant part of an organizational structure, and that senior managers often attempt to liberate the creativity of their organizations by dispensing with middle managers altogether. Nonaka and Takeuchi see this impatience with the middle level of management as understandable but mistaken. Middle managers, they suggest, are a fundamental part of the mechanism by which an organization can manage and develop knowledge. They are the meeting points where knowledge from different parts of the organization converge; potentially, they can be the prime movers in spotting opportunities for innovation and fostering creative projects.

CASE STUDY

THE UGLY DUCKLING SYNDROME – ORGANIZATIONAL TRANSFORMATION AT HUMBERSIDE TEC

Peter Fryer was Chief Executive of Humberside TEC (Technology and Enterprise Council) in the north of England from its beginning. He is an avid student of learning organizations and is keen on applying ideas from chaos theory and complexity to the way organizations work. And not just any organization: Peter took the risk of applying his ideas in the TEC itself.

Until recently, TECs existed to promote skills training for businesses in their local communities. Peter sought to create, inside his own organization, a working environment that was both challenging and rewarding. His enthusiasm is infectious. Sit down with him and before long he will start showing you lists. 'Look at these,' he says, pushing a list of 'essential business processes' under your nose.

- Business plans
- Rules, systems and procedures
- Organization charts

- Job descriptions
- Budgets
- Communications.

These look like the stuff of normal organizational life; yet something tells you that Fryer is about to say something uncomfortable. 'What do we all know about these processes? That they don't work. We try to make them work, but, by and large, they don't. They all tend to be organized around the worst case. Who's the biggest idiot around here, and how do we construct systems and job descriptions that even they could understand?'

Fryer is convinced that these systems merely develop people's stupidity. And at Humberside TEC he dispensed with them. In their place, he put three key notions.

- Responsible adults
- Trust
- Support.

If you create an organization that functions as a complex adaptive system, he argues, then people will behave accordingly. So he encouraged people to make connections: anyone could talk to anyone, everyone was responsible for being communicated with and networking was the order of the day. People were encouraged to learn: to 'love mistakes to death', in Fryer's words, seeing them as an opportunity to learn. 'Learning is the process by which we co-evolve with our environment,' he says, invoking the language of complexity theory. 'And the best learning is learning by doing.'

Fryer also saw the business processes within the TEC as living and continually developing. 'Planning and evaluation are continuous; the systems were based on our best people and the outcomes we were looking for; structures should follow and not lead.' Fryer encouraged the formation of self-organizing teams and firmly discouraged downward management. 'People were encouraged to get the job done without asking. We didn't have a suggestion scheme, for example. If someone had an idea, we said to them, "Don't tell us about it. Just do it."'

Fryer likes to quote Sir John Harvey-Jones on planning. 'Planning is an unnatural process; it's much more fun to do something. And the nicest thing about not planning is that failure comes as a complete surprise rather than being preceded by a period of worry and depression.'

Fryer sees change management as a continuous responsibility of everybody in the organization. Instead of a single huge change, which he dubs the 'Trojan Horse' approach, he offers 'Trojan Mice': small changes made every day, so that they are small enough for the system to assimilate. He sees an organization as being like an amoeba; very simple in its construction. An amoeba has a central core and a highly sensitive surface. If it senses danger, cells on the surface communicate immediately with the centre and demand resource to change shape or move. The activity of the amoeba is determined by the cells that interface with its environment. 'That's what an organization should be like. The people who work at the interface should change the organization's direction.'

But doesn't that make for a lot of stressed-out people? 'Not at Humberside it didn't. We had very few days lost through stress. In fact, this way of doing things removes stress, because people feel in charge of their lives.'

And does this way of running an organization work? 'Well, by all the normal measures of success, we did very well.'

The government abolished all TECs in 2001. Peter is now an independent consultant, working with a wide range of organizations and with the London School of Economics. His passion for his ideas remains undimmed. He invokes Hans Christian Andersen to sum up his approach. 'Many people in business are frustrated that, no matter how hard they try to control their workforce and their actions, no matter how many rules, procedures and structures they impose, they are still surprised by the unpredictable. They're convinced that they've got an ugly duckling, and they want to make it beautiful. Actually, what they've got isn't a duck at all; it's a beautiful swan. If they could see that, they would realize that by trying to control their workforce they are suppressing a powerful force – the imagination and ingenuity of their people – and they would also realize that knowledge is not a "thing" to be managed but an ecology to be nurtured.'

Perhaps it is largely a matter of recognizing the current position of an enterprise and finding the managerial structures and processes that are best suited to it. But innovation is not 'something in the air'. It is not an attitude of mind to be fostered either by environmental improvements or changes in managerial structure. Innovation is a process; like any other process, it must be managed. Organizations must establish systems and procedures to give innovation the discipline that any structured and organized work demands. Without them, innovation simply won't happen. In the next chapter, we examine some of these systems and ways of modelling the innovation process.

Managing the process of innovation

Managing innovation is complicated. It rarely proceeds in a straight line. Difficult questions arise at every stage of the process. At the start: Where to look for new ideas? How to know which ideas are worth pursuing? As the process continues: How to develop those ideas into feasible products or services? How to know when a project needs more resource? When to abandon a project before it consumes too much resource? How to manage the innovators? As the project nears completion: How to ensure that innovations become integrated into existing processes and strategies? Or perhaps, how to adapt the wider strategies of the organization to accommodate the innovation?

But the real test of any innovation is whether it succeeds in the organization's environment. Does it make a difference to clients, partners or users? Does it create a new source of customer satisfaction? How do you measure that success? The impact of an innovation can be impossible to predict. Antibiotics were an almost immediate and overwhelming success. By contrast, the steam engine was something of a slow starter. A working model of a steam turbine was invented by Hero of Alexandria in AD62. But the innovation did not take off in a civilization that enjoyed almost unlimited slave labour and had no need for mechanical power.

Most innovations fail. The unpredictability of innovation means that any innovation strategy must plan for a low success rate. 'The mortality rate of innovations,' says Peter Drucker, 'is – and should be – high.' An innovation strategy that fails to recognize this simple fact will probably itself fail.

All of this makes managing innovation a profoundly uncomfortable prospect for many managers. Yet it is precisely because innovation is unpredictable that it must be carefully managed. Innovation is work and, like all work, it must be organized; but it demands a particular kind of management.

INNOVATION AND OPERATION – TWO CYCLES

Operational and innovative work exist in a dynamic relationship. All work should have these two dimensions to be satisfying and productive. Innovative work makes operational work worth doing; operational work offers a secure foundation for innovation to happen. It's hard work being creative if the essential housekeeping hasn't been done. Innovative work feeds back into operational work, making it more productive, efficient and enjoyable. Operational work with no prospect of anything new is drudgery; creative work that never achieves anything in the real world is daydreaming.

These two dimensions of work have become separated in the modern workplace. In pre-industrial work, they coexist: the craftsman's life is devoted to understanding how operational skill can support creative flair. The demands of industrialization – and of its administrative cousin, bureaucracy – split the two kinds of work apart. Operational work became organized functionally and allocated to 'hired hands'; creative work – deciding on strategy, choosing which products to develop, looking for new markets – was the job of 'management', organized typically not by function but as a single team or board.

Innovation and operational work recombine, perhaps, in the mind of the entrepreneur – but the tension between the two, even for a single individual, can sometimes be less than creative.

We cannot do operational and innovative work *at the same time*. They have different aims. The demands, thinking, activities and resources for each are different. The two cycles complement each other, and even link at one point; but they are *separate*.

OPERATIONAL AND INNOVATIVE WORK CYCLES

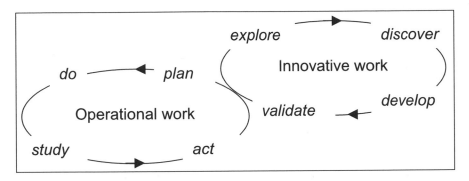

Operational work is the work we do to continue doing what we always do. It is the cycle where most of us do most of our work. At its simplest, it describes ordinary, functional, maintenance or day-to-day work. It operates according to certain standards, rules and routines. We might develop it into a cycle of continuous improvement. The lower cycle in this diagram is based on Dr Deming's famous 'PDSA' cycle, much beloved of problem solvers and managers involved in quality initiatives.

The cycle involves four stages.

- **Plan** – to do something, to change something or test a process.
- **Do** – what you planned to do, make the change or do the test.
- **Study** – the results: What worked well? What went wrong? What have you learned?
- **Act** – set out to do it differently, adopt the change, or abandon it, or run it again, or adapt it to new learning.

The key feature of this cycle is that it repeats itself. One cycle of improvement feeds into others. It is as much a model of learning as of operational activity. The aim of the cycle is to maintain or improve a process or system that already exists.

The innovation cycle, by contrast, seeks to create something new. Its four distinctive features are drawn – with some minor changes – from Alfred Wallas' model of creativity.

- **Explore** – look elsewhere; invoke curiosity; simply see what we can find.
- **Discover** – something interesting, as defined by some broad set of criteria.
- **Develop** – take the discovery and work on it to create something useful.
- **Validate** – test the new discovery for feasibility.

The innovation cycle is a journey into unknown territory. As mentioned in the Introduction, this journey is memorably summarized by Joseph Campbell, the mythographer. 'Creativity,' wrote Campbell, 'consists in going out to find the thing society hasn't found yet.' The journey involves risk: we may find nothing of any interest; we may even put ourselves in danger. Like any self-respecting explorer, we must embark on our journey well prepared. The discoveries we may make will be interesting because they relate to some set of values, interests or priorities that we bring with us. A car-maker, for example, may be particularly interested in discovering objects or organisms that travel efficiently, or use fuel in unexpected ways, and so on. A health administrator might take a particular interest in social groups that manage their own health in new ways, that use new sources of medication or manage unhealthy behaviour in an unexpected manner. Once made, the discoveries have to be brought back into our own world as something of use. This may mean developing them and testing them to make sure that they would work or survive in our circumstances.

CRISIS OR CHOICE – MAKING THE MOVE INTO INNOVATIVE THINKING

There are two reasons for embarking on such a journey. Either we have to, or we choose to. A crisis may precipitate a burst of creativity – or, at least, a frantic search for new ideas. Generally, however, we are not at our most creative in times of crisis; and, by the time the crisis has hit, it may be too late. On the other hand, we could *choose* to 'go innovative': we could deliberately decide to leave the operational cycle for a while and enter the cycle of innovation.

This decision *must* be deliberate. It's best made at the 'act' point of the operational cycle: after studying the effects of past actions and realizing that they are no longer suitable or adequate for new circumstances. Bringing an innovation back into the operational cycle must be timed with care. It must be integrated into forward plans so that it has a chance of surviving and the rest of the operation is disrupted as little as necessary.

The critical point is this: we must *decide* to innovate; it won't just happen.

CONFUSING OPERATIONAL AND INNOVATIVE WORK

Many of the misunderstandings surrounding innovation arise from the fundamental inability to distinguish it from operational work. For example, directors often express bafflement at the lack of creativity in their organizations. Their dismay is based on a number of assumptions:

- that creativity is desirable in the workforce;
- that the operational workforce can and should be the source of innovation in the organization; and
- that the same staff who are working heroically to keep the organization functioning have the motivation or energy to be creative.

Managers often assume that creativity and innovation are one and the same thing; that both activities are in some way 'natural' and 'spontaneous'; and that, if they are not 'naturally' occurring in an organization, something must be 'stifling' them. Remove the barriers – better still, motivate people by rewarding creativity – and new ideas will spring forth miraculously, like water from a rock.

These assumptions may be false. An organization's need for creativity depends on its mission and the work needed to accomplish it. Creativity is no more or less 'natural' than a desire for security; innovation is no more spontaneous than habit. People *choose* to create. And organizations must *choose* to innovate. If innovation is not part of an organization's strategy – and if the organization fails to find a place for innovation within its structure – then the people working in it are unlikely to see any reason to be creative. Innovation will continue to be seen as the preserve of the maverick, the outsider or the subversive. And creativity will be perceived as a threat to the stability and security of the organization.

THE PERILS OF INNOVATION

Trying to innovate can be a bad career move. A five-year study by a group of faculty members at the Rensselaer Polytechnic Institute in New York State tracked 12 innovation projects in ten large companies. Of 12 project leaders, four resigned, two threatened to resign and two were dismissed.

This stress, the researchers found, derives largely from false expectations on the part of the host organization. The success ethic can damage innovators' motivation and self-confidence. The source of a successful innovation may be forgotten; nobody ever forgets a major failure. Senior management may fail to understand that innovators tend to be technically proficient but lacking in the skills to sell the business benefits of an idea. Some may not even see the benefits until someone else points them out. Some companies, apparently, claim to welcome new ideas but lack the systems to support them. Or they ignore an innovative idea because it doesn't fit into existing business units.

This inability to find a place for innovation within an organization can become translated into political or behavioural manoeuvring. Precisely because the structure has no place for them, innovators tend to be viewed as 'irritating viruses' in the host organization (the organic metaphor is telling). In one project, 'the usual organizational antibodies were applied in an attempt to neutralize it: withholding of funding, general nay-saying and subtle signals that it might not be "career smart" to associate with the project.'

FINDING A PLACE FOR INNOVATION

Innovative work, then, must be separated from operational work, and protected from it. Peter Drucker is uncompromising about this. 'Do not,' he orders, 'make innovation an objective for people charged with running, exploiting or optimizing what already exists.'

Separating innovative work from operational work creates a number of imperatives in any organization.

IMPERATIVES FOR AN INNOVATION STRATEGY

✓ **Organize innovation separately.** Depending on the size of the organization, it may be made the responsibility of a single manager, a team, a department or even an independent business.

✓ **Integrate innovation into the organization's policies and practices.** Innovation on the side rarely works.

✓ **Innovate, don't diversify.** Attempting to create something new in one's own field is hard enough, without trying to innovate elsewhere.

✓ **Place responsibility for innovation high in the organization.** Someone in senior management must take on the specific assignment of developing new ideas.

✓ **Budget for innovation separately.** Innovation objectives need to be set differently from operational ones. The rules need to be different. What sorts of policy, rules and measurements should apply? What disciplines to impose on them? People should not be rewarded for failure; but neither should they be penalized for taking risks. And the returns should be measured differently. What are the appropriate time spans? When to scale up, when to pull the plug? The answers will depend on the nature of the business. The risk of innovation is unavoidable; for that very reason, it should be carefully managed.

✓ **Make sure that the person or unit in charge of innovation is clearly accountable.** It is through accountability that the innovating unit finds its place in the larger organization.

CASE STUDY

TOWARDS THE THIRD HORIZON – DIFFERENTIATING INNOVATION AT IBM

IBM has learnt the lessons of its troubled past. It had failed to conquer major markets in the computing industry; now an initiative at the corporation aims to sharpen its management of new ideas.

Partly, it's a problem of the speed of technological change. Getting a massive organization to respond quickly to new developments is particularly difficult. Responsibility starts at the very top. The job has been given to John Thompson, IBM's Vice Chairman. He has a growth target of 10% on annual sales of $90bn. 'That's like creating an Oracle every year,' he says. No easy task.

The process starts, typically perhaps for a business famed for its bureaucracy, with centralized reviews of market trends and technology developments. Out of these comes a list of promising new ideas that IBM turns into new businesses: units developing data networking equipment, for example. These are 'Horizon Three' operations – distinct from 'Horizon One' (mature businesses) or 'Horizon Two' (growth businesses that extend existing operations). Horizon Three businesses are more like start-ups.

Thompson is fully aware of the need for an eagle eye in managing these opportunities: 'New businesses sometimes fall in the white spaces between organizational boundaries,' he says. Sometimes they even conflict with existing business units. So they need to be managed differently, and protected from the pressures of the corporate giant that has spawned them.

Thompson sees his task as getting the best people onto the job and keeping them there. His strategy has three main planks.

- **Separate the business from normal operations.** 'In the past,' says Thompson, 'we've added it to someone's portfolio' – and the result has typically been failure. Each project has a dedicated team.

- **Insulate new businesses from traditional management and accounting methods.** No detailed financial plans or reviews; broad revenue and investment targets are the norm.

- **Give support from the top.** Middle managers with the power to block new projects must see that senior management are active sponsors. 'The days are gone,' states Thompson bullishly, 'when a manager down in the trenches can decide "I don't like that project".'

This personal protection and support seems to be vital. Without it, problems may escalate and projects may flounder.

But John Thompson will only be around to give that personal leadership for another couple of years. Will these new initiatives survive when he has gone?

OPERATIONAL WORK – FUNCTIONAL STRUCTURE

Operational work generates a functional organizational structure. Functional organizations structure work in stages, and by related skills. Processes are broken down into parts, with each functional section completing a part. Other functions – human resources (HR), finance – are organized by skill, or according to their general supporting function.

A functional organizational structure strikingly resembles Steven Mithen's 'cathedral of the mind', as discussed in Chapter 1. Just as the mind is made up of a central, general thinking area surrounded by 'chapels' of specialized thinking domains, so our organizations tend to be constructed as specialized functions supported by a generalized administrative base. Perhaps we structure organizations functionally because we tend to organize our thinking in the same way.

This functional arrangement has a number of advantages. Because the work 'moves' through functions and functional workers perform the same function repeatedly, people tend to know clearly what is expected of them. The structure gives them stability and the opportunity to develop their functional skills. They can focus their effort. The resulting efficiencies are a definite economic benefit. Because the work is more or less exactly defined, it can be measured and standards applied.

But this way of structuring work creates some difficulties. It tends to create 'silo' working: functionaries find it hard to see how their work fits into the larger scheme. Friction and misunderstandings between functions are common. The structure is inflexible: if the structure of the work changes, it is a major task to change the organizational structure. Functional working limits 'learning for tomorrow': people are encouraged to develop only the skills necessary for their function.

Above all, a functional structure is inappropriate for innovation. It is designed to fulfil operational work; and innovation has no place in operational work. It disrupts operational consistency. And not just when the operation is prone to break down. Obviously, a functional manager suffering the stress of operating difficulties will hardly welcome a new idea that promises only further disruption. But the greatest enemy of innovation is the *successful* operation. That success was probably hard-won; to threaten it with new-fangled ideas will seem, to the operational manager, frankly stupid.

To judge the innovative idea by operational standards is almost certainly to condemn it at birth.

---

20 IDEA KILLERS

First, don't blame the murderer. These 'idea killers' are obvious and often reasonable operational responses to a new idea. If you want to nurture new ideas, you must take them *away* from the operational, day-to-day running of the organization. You must switch disciplines: from the systems, routines and measurements of operational thinking to the very different disciplines of innovative thinking.

Not practical.

It'll never work.

Let's wait a bit.

Too complicated.

What's the point?

That reminds me...

It'll cost too much.

It'll never catch on.

What about the intangibles?

You haven't thought it through.

We tried it before and it didn't work.

That's a bit too radical for this company.

You'll never get people to change their ways.

I like the idea, but I'm not sure that my boss...

That isn't really the way we do things around here.

The idea isn't relevant to our current strategic plan.

Good idea. We'll appoint a working party to look into it.

Of course, that's just the sort of idea we might expect from *you*.

Hm. Now, suppose we changed this little bit, and that little bit, and...

We don't have the resources/staff/money/time/expertise/room/systems...

INNOVATION WORK – PROJECT STRUCTURE

Innovation work demands a different organizational structure from operational work. Where operational work breaks a task into stages, innovation demands that the work be considered as a complete task. Where operational work organizes people into functional units, innovation work demands a multi-functional team. An operational task moves through a number of functions that remain fixed within the organizational structure; an innovation task, in contrast, remains where it is, and a team made up of different skills moves to it.

What might such a structure look like? In Mithen's 'cathedral of the mind', innovation arises when the walls between specialized 'chapels' or cognitive domains are opened and ideas can travel between them. Mithen posits a 'superchapel' where the mental contents of one domain can combine with ideas from another. The 'chapels' of functional work are the functional departments. What might be the organizational equivalent of a 'superchapel'?

The obvious answer is: a project. Projects, by definition, are self-contained units of work, separately budgeted and managed, set up to deliver a specific result. They are eminently suitable vehicles for innovation. A project organizes the work as a separate unit while allowing the organization to integrate it into its wider strategy. It allows the work to be separately budgeted and managed, with a project manager accountable for the 'deliverables'. The task has a better chance of being achieved because

TWO KINDS OF WORK

1 Functional structure
(the work 'moves'; bundles of related skills)

Advantages
✓ Clarity of work
✓ Stability
✓ Improves functional skill
✓ Economy
✓ Effort focus
✓ Standards

Problems
✗ Difficult to see whole task
✗ Lack of flexibility
✗ Limits learning for tomorrow
✗ Friction; misunderstandings

2 Project structure
(the work 'stays still'; broad mission; different complete tasks; diverse skills and knowledge)

Advantages
✓ Responsibility for whole task
✓ Flexibility
✓ Encourages learning
✓ Ideal for innovation

Problems
✗ Unclear mission?
✗ Instability
✗ Much housekeeping
✗ Need for teambuilding
✗ Isolation from environment
✗ Limited by size

the team has complete responsibility for the whole job. A project is flexible: once the task is complete – or if it must be abandoned – the team can simply be disbanded. Project working encourages real learning, as each new task brings its own unique challenges.

There are, of course, potential problems. The nature of the task might not be clear. Flexibility is also instability: people may need extra support or a greater sense of self-sufficiency to survive. Team work demands enormous amounts of 'housekeeping' and teambuilding: people need to know what is expected of them, and how their work fits into the wider project; the identity of the team needs to be maintained continually. The project is likely to become isolated from the rest of the organization, losing its sense of perspective or relevance to wider strategic objectives.

Such work is also limited by team size: major innovation projects involving more than a score of people will become particularly hard to manage.

MATRIX MANAGEMENT

The common consequence of project management, within an organization structured functionally, is 'matrix management'. A project manager takes on full responsibility for performance, costs and timescales. Members of the project team are assigned part- or full-time to the project and find themselves the servants of two masters: their functional manager and the project manager.

Some might say that matrix management is almost designed to create friction. Project managers must be able to influence functional managers who are not answerable to them. They may well be competing with other project managers for the same resources. They may also have difficulty motivating people to commit to the project. Team members may be spending only a part of their time on a project; they may be answerable to other project managers and to their functional line manager. They may know other team members a little or not at all, and feel insecure about their future when the project ends. The job of project manager is one of the most demanding around.

THE INDEPENDENT PROJECT ORGANIZATION

One way to square the circle of matrix management is to isolate the project within a separate organization. In an independent project organization (IPO), the project manager becomes more like a managing director and reports to the head of the parent company. Members of the new organization may be recruited from the parent or brought in from outside, as employees, associates or consultants. Such commitment to an independent organization, however, may isolate it from the parent company. It may also be harder to cancel the project if a whole organizational structure has been established to support it.

THE VENTURE TEAM

In recent years, a variation on the IPO has appeared on the scene. A venture team is often a small project team supported by the parent company as an 'intrapreneurial' venture. The team must justify investment in the project to a managing group within the parent company and any functional units from whom they want to take resource or expertise. The company makes a limited investment in the venture and guarantees to support it through development and into the market. The company's name, experience and support in key business areas can allow the innovators to concentrate on the idea; in return, the intrapreneurs must be willing to sacrifice a level of return in any success.

CASE STUDY

GOING TO THE PUB FOR INSPIRATION – VENTURE PARTNER-SHIPS AT SIX CONTINENTS RETAIL

Six Continents Retail (formerly part of Bass Breweries) has been developing new brands in a novel partnership between corporate strength and entrepreneurial flair.

Traditional Bass pubs – on the housing estates of the Midlands and the north of England – were flagging badly during the 1990s. Tim Clarke, at that time Chief Executive of Bass Leisure Retail, saw the need for what he calls 'a radical break-out strategy of new product development and concept innovation.' So he and other senior executives went pubbing, and talent-spotting.

They found two young entrepreneurs and persuaded them to come and work with the group for a fixed period, in exchange for a share of any profits if the ventures succeeded.

Amanda Wilmott developed All Bar One, an upmarket, female-friendly chain of bars that has opened 50 city centre outlets in the past six years. And David Lee created It's a Scream, 75 bars located in student venues.

Clarke thinks that mixing individual enterprise and the clout of a major brewery has been a major success. 'They've had the personal satisfaction of expressing their creativity, which is very important to them,' he says. 'We take ownership of the brand and the intellectual property, but they have corporate cashflow behind them and an extremely attractive earnout.'

Six Continents has replicated this business model with other brands, like Vintage Inns, Harvester, Toby, Browns, O'Neill's, Edwards, Ember Inns and Goose. Aspiring entrepreneurs within the company can find themselves taken off regular duties and sponsored to put their ideas into practice. These new brands are now contributing over 30% of turnover.

Clarke emphasizes the need for senior support for ventures of this kind.

'We spend two or three nights a week out and about in the business,' he adds, 'understanding where the creative ideas are and tying them back in with the formal process of consumer market research.' So creativity and innovation also become integrated into Six Continents' overall strategy.

RESEARCH AND DEVELOPMENT – INSTITUTIONALIZING INNOVATION

The earliest, and by now the best established, vehicle for innovation within organizations is the research and development laboratory.

The term 'R&D' often refers only to long-range research work. It is in this area that 'blue-sky' research explores new ideas without any pre-conceived relationship to a product or application. These ideas may then be passed on to a product engineering team to apply them in products: a process often referred to as 'phased hand-out'.

The danger, of course, is that the 'pure research' teams become detached from the organization's overall strategy or the needs of customers. Some companies have therefore brought the two functions together: 'pure' ideas and product applications are developed in parallel, albeit often in separate units.

Rajesh Nellore, Head of Strategic Planning in group global purchasing at Electrolux, has drawn a complete schematic of today's R&D process.

Nellore identifies *three* main components of modern R&D.

THREE MAIN COMPONENTS

1 **Long-range research**, generating ideas with no view to an application.
2 **Advanced product engineering**, directed at specific products and applications in other product lines. Advanced product engineering develops concepts that are product-specific but might be matched with other concepts to create new products.
3 **Product engineering** or **release engineering**. Product engineers take the concepts that advanced product engineers produce and adapt them for specific products.

Smaller companies may not separate the two engineering functions. 'This is also common,' says Nellore, 'in industries where the rate of innovation is low and the emphasis is more on developing existing knowledge.'

LEADING TO MARKET – THE PLACE OF R&D IN INNOVATION MANAGEMENT

Recent research by PA Consulting suggests that spending more on R&D doesn't necessarily lead to more innovation.

The agency talked to directors in 150 UK companies. The companies that spent the most on R&D proved to be getting the least return on their investment. 'Although they have much larger R&D budgets in absolute terms, they spend much less of them on really innovative products,' claims John Buckley, PA's Head of Technology. 'The leaders of smaller companies are showing more vision and leadership and fostering a creative culture.' Indeed, a clear vision and committed leadership from the top seemed to be one of the most important elements in making innovation happen.

The successful innovators also put far more emphasis on the marketplace. Is innovation a technological issue or a customer issue? Buckley himself is in no doubt. 'Far too many companies are trying to focus on the product,' he states. 'If I am a shareholder in a food company, do I want them spending my investment on basic research or getting a better product onto the market faster? I think it should be the latter. Innovation is a chief executive issue, not just an R&D issue.'

MODELS OF THE INNOVATION PROCESS

Organized innovation demands discipline. Organizations are extremely unlikely to throw resources at a project unquestioningly. The project team needs to know what they are working towards, and how they should best do the job.

The simplest model of the innovation process breaks it into two stages.

- **The 'creative' stage** – having or generating ideas.
- **The 'application' stage** – putting the ideas to work in practical ways.

Models often introduce a middle stage in which ideas are developed: feasibility is 'built in' to an idea in an attempt to make it more viable in operational terms. The 'advanced product engineering' department within the R&D process, for example, exists to develop 'pure' research into potential product lines or components. Thus, the archetypal organizational model of the innovation process is a sequence of three steps:

- idea generation or capture;
- idea development; and
- commercialization or implementation.

Project management models – and the commercially available software based on them – usually follow these three stages, sometimes in more sophisticated forms.

Nellore sees a danger inherent in this compartmentalized approach. The more hand-outs between R&D departments, the greater the difference is likely to be between planned and actual products. What's more, problems in the application stage – of adapting innovations to existing products, or building feasibility into a new product – will tend not to feed *back* across departmental boundaries to incorporation in future work. In other words, the sequential model of R&D often fails to allow researchers to *learn*.

It is this lack of 'lateral integration' that can weaken the stepwise approach of traditional R&D. Innovation cannot take place in a chaotic environment; but neither can it flourish in a rigid structure where ideas are 'thrown over the wall' rather than worked on collaboratively.

NEWPROD – A STAGE MODEL OF INNOVATION

Robert Cooper, a Canadian researcher, has developed one of the best known models of the innovation process based on the archetypal three-stage model. 'NewProd' incorporates impressive work that Cooper carried out in the 1980s to identify the factors that made for successful innovations. Cooper sampled about one hundred new products, some successful, others less so. He found that a small number of key factors seemed to predict success. The top three were what he called *product advantage, proficiency of pre-development activities* and *protocol.*

- **Product advantage.** The new product offered unique features to the customer, was of higher quality than any competitive product, reduced the customer's costs or benefited the customer in some unique way.
- **Proficiency of pre-development activities.** 'Up-front' activities were well managed. These include initial screening of the project; preliminary market and technical assessments; market research and financial analysis.
- **Protocol.** Before the project began to develop the product, the team had clearly defined the target market, customers' needs, wants and preferences, the product concept and broad specifications and requirements of the finished innovation.

Cooper then builds these factors into the project model and makes these important points.

Product advantage to the customer is of prime importance. The number one objective of any innovation product must be to create a product that the customer sees as having *real* advantages, in terms of benefit, quality, cost, newness, superiority or ability to solve a problem. Any innovation that can't demonstrate that it is aiming to beat the competition on all of these six factors must focus effort on them. And key to this work must be research into customer needs and preferences: the project must be able to demonstrate that customers *genuinely* want what the innovation promises to deliver.

Project definition and up-front activities are vital. 'The most critical steps in the new product process,' says Cooper, 'are those that occur *before* the product development gets underway.' Management must be prepared to devote resources to market research, technical assessments, financial analysis and initial screening. They should be built in to the innovation process as routine. And they should lead to a clear definition of the project in terms of its target market, customers' needs, the benefits delivered by the product and its specification.

Synergy is a key factor in success. The project should have a good 'fit' with the company's strategy and current operations. The marketing and sales people should feel comfortable with the innovation, as should the technicians who will need to develop and produce it. Innovation projects must include conversations between all the functions involved, throughout the process, rather than 'throwing ideas over the wall'.

One of the most interesting conclusions of Cooper's work is that the success of an innovation project is largely determined by factors within the project manager's control. These include:

- pre-development;
- market-related activity;
- technical work;
- developing unique features and benefits in the product; and
- getting the protocol right.

Cooper's checklists help the project manager to manage the unpredictability of innovation. Innovation is always a journey of exploration; innovation projects can – and often do – alter course. When the explorers get lost, Cooper's model suggests where the project team might look to maximize the chances of success.

The alchemical marriage – integrating opposites in innovation management

SARAH LLOYD-JONES

Sarah Lloyd-Jones read music at university and went on to join Unilever. She worked in marketing until 1996, leading the development and launch of the PG Tips pyramid teabag. She then became Company Innovation Manager for Van den Bergh Foods. She recently became Innovation Champion for Unilever's Foods and Beverages Europe division. Sarah is also involved in psychodynamic counselling and runs marathons in her spare time.

Innovation is full of conflicts and opposites. Marrying these opposites is a central challenge for anybody seeking to manage innovation. Both team leaders and managers sponsoring teams must find ways of reconciling the 'hard' and 'soft' elements in innovation. In this chapter, we will explore these elements and how we might start to integrate them into a management philosophy.

Innovation is exciting. It brings with it thoughts about creativity and the heady world of ideas. Innovation is partly about dreams.

But then there is reality. There is the frustration when we meet difficulties and must recast our expectations. There are unwelcome intrusions: the corporate landscape is full of people changing jobs and shifting political agendas. There are long timescales and the need for patience. There are moments of not knowing and feelings of wandering around in the dark; there are agonizing decisions and sometimes the need to cope with failure, to learn hard lessons.

So innovation is fascinating, problematic and contrary. Unless we can understand and integrate the seemingly opposing forces at play, we will remain rigidly in one position or lurch catastrophically from one side to the other.

PROJECTS AND THE DECISION-MAKING PROCESS – AN EXAMPLE OF OPPOSITES

Organizations manage investment decisions differently, according to how large they are. In a very small company, people might not need documentation and round table meetings as they know what's going on and what is at stake. In a large company, things are entirely different; it will take time – and an efficient and transparent process – to debate and communicate decisions well.

A company with a portfolio of innovation projects will face many of these decisions. The relevant team needs to be involved in the decision, to reach the right outcome as often as possible. Typically, a company such as Unilever will use a stage-gate process something like the 'funnel and gates' model evolved at Harvard. In a major project, there will be three or four critical points at which the project team produces a decision paper with their recommendation and supporting arguments, increasingly specific at each stage about evidence, risks and the business case. Checklists sometimes accompany the funnel to help the team plan and run the project well, and to prepare good decision papers.

Commitment of resources to a project increases at each of these 'gates'. Projects that don't live up to the initial hopes must be weeded out so that precious resource is only put behind projects that fit the company strategy and are a good enough bet.

Senior managers with experience of innovation often install this type of decision-making process as the first element of the innovation process. They have seen enough resource spent on projects that were wrong for the company, too poorly executed or financially unsound. Usually these 'old hands' like to see risk being managed (not avoided), not because they imagine 100% success is possible but because they like to see the *right* risks being taken.

To these 'gatekeepers' the decision process represents:

- clarity and strategic focus;
- control of resource;
- collective ownership by the business;
- risk management;
- objectivity and reflection;
- time taken over important issues;
- input from experienced and naive minds; and
- unequivocal and passionate commitment.

The trouble comes when a resource allocation/decision process is presented as 'the total innovation process'.

Put yourself in the shoes of an enthusiastic new recruit to management. Your expectations and excitement are high. You see innovation as the most exciting arena in the organization, somewhere to roll up your sleeves and get thoroughly immersed. You are likely to see innovation as being about creativity and entrepreneurial spirit. You may have idealistic hopes that your ideas will be attended to and appreciated. After all, your ideas are good, and you may well believe that you were recruited for them. What you expect from the company is the freedom and encouragement to pursue them.

Imagine, then, that the first innovation training course you attend is all about discipline, preparation and risk management (sounds like risk avoidance), with bosses 'marking the papers'. It's back to exams and feeling controlled, or so it might seem. Now imagine that the 'gate' process has been implemented in a soulless and uninspiring way. Maybe the gatekeepers don't communicate their criteria for decisions; maybe the gatekeepers themselves aren't fully agreed on the goal posts. Perhaps the project team of which you are a member is impatient to get on and doesn't see the need for reflection and objectivity. Now the new recruit's view of the process will be:

- red tape and time wasted on papers;
- *fait accompli*, the decision is already made;

- loss of momentum, 'dead' time for the project;
- interference and unwanted control;
- nit-picking and restriction of creativity;
- 'Why didn't they tell us this earlier?';
- loss of ownership;
- politics, hidden agenda;
- the worst meeting in the calendar; and
- outputs not clear.

Their satisfaction at work will be overshadowed by the sense of a stifling and uncreative environment. They are likely to feel the loss of some of their personal ideals and expectations.

Of course, things may not be so bad. The climate in the company may be far more balanced. Maybe the 'stage gates' are presented in an integrated way, with respect for creativity and passion, and with total alignment to the major decisions made on projects. Is innovation about freedom and creativity, or is it about judgement? The tension will be there somewhere, whether inside people or between them.

Why? Because the tension is a creative one and has to be.

TWO WORLDS

So innovation isn't a homogenous process, but a combination of two worlds. Let us consider these more closely.

1 THE 'FEELING' WORLD OF CREATIVITY AND 'SOFT' ELEMENTS

The world of ideas and creativity is a world of feeling. Ideas come from the playful, instinctive, experimental, childlike parts of ourselves. Our creativity relies on our being able to let go and just be, in an uncontrolled and spontaneous way, and to investigate the impulses and ideas that arise.

Growing up erodes the child's world of limitless freedom. At a practical level, children have to learn how to stay alive and live productively in a dangerous world. This means not playing with some really interesting toys like hot cookers or electricity sockets, and not exploring main roads in spite of a host of fascinating shapes, noises and smells. It means

THE FEELING WORLD OF CREATIVITY

Is about

Creativity, new ideas

An instinctive approach

Inclusiveness, making links

Being open to possibilities

Freedom

Personal feelings, subjectivity

Personal belief, passion, personal motivation

Spontaneous expression

Needs

Understanding

Recognition and more recognition

Patience

taking responsibility for time and learning how to become independent; realizing the painful truth that other people are separate beings with their own needs; and learning that the resources available to meet all the needs are limited. We learn from past experience to live and think within limits. Maintaining the inner child may not be easy. Picasso famously said that it took him 60 years to learn to see like a child.

In the feeling world, instincts have free rein in our imagination and our expression. We value impulses and explore them to see where they might lead. The habit of judging things as good or bad has to be put aside temporarily to make this possible. Spontaneity has to be rehearsed; one of the many contradictions in innovation.

Visualize two axes. On the vertical axis we have thoughts about value. Words like good, bad, better, worse, right, wrong and judgement come in here. On the horizontal axis come questions like 'What is it like?'; 'What does it mean?' and 'What comes next?' An idea needs to be explored, developed and have breadth (lateral thought) before being placed on the good/bad scale. The question is how much effort to invest in exploration before comparing the idea with others (vertical thought) and making choices.

EVALUATION VS EXPLORATION AXIS

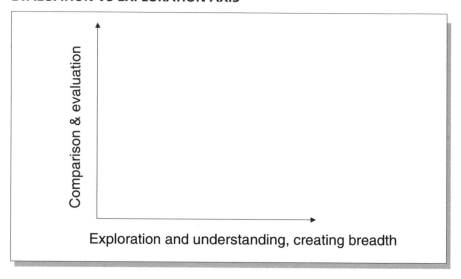

We invest a good deal of ourselves in our ideas. They come from a vulnerable part of ourselves. If an idea gets judged, the person gets judged too, always with a risk of damage to the creative self. Judgement may be necessary, but it will be far more constructive if it follows a good exploration that recognizes the idea's potential. Ideas, and people, need to be recognized and encouraged.

2 THE 'RATIONAL' WORLD OF JUDGEMENT AND 'HARD' ELEMENTS
The other world is an adult world of learning. The creative world is partly about selective unlearning, the rational world about things we must learn. Thought can be the enemy of creativity if it replaces feeling and the creative impulse, or it can be the facilitating container that surrounds feelings and ideas.

Time and money are finite. There is never enough of either for every wish or idea, in life or in business. It is in the rational world that choices

THE RATIONAL WORLD OF JUDGEMENT

Is about

Practicality, realism

Discipline, thoroughness

Focus, purpose, articulation

Limits, exclusions, structure

Evidence, measurement, objectivity

Evaluation, comparison, choice, either/or

Planning, use of resource

Judgement

Needs

Clarity, transparency and precision

Effort, method and discipline

Occasional ruthlessness

have to be made. As projects approach launch, they need more and more thoroughness, discipline and risk management. Although the idea and the alternatives presented at each decision point come from the creative world, the task is to sift out the subjective elements as far as possible from the data.

It's almost impossible to distil the soft elements from decision making and, indeed, it is undesirable. If we look back at idea generation, the reverse is also true. Creativity needs a purpose; idea generation work needs a clear enough brief, a framework to contain it. The two worlds are confusing: they exist in parallel and we must deal in both, skilfully, most of the time.

HARD AND SOFT ELEMENTS IN THE INNOVATION PROCESS

Let us consider the key elements of the innovation process.

KEY ELEMENTS OF THE INNOVATION PROCESS

STRATEGY AND PORTFOLIO MANAGEMENT

Strategy contains innovation and gives it a sense of direction. This means agreeing criteria for making choices. Whether our strategy is tightly defined or looser, it will call both on soft elements:

- creative thinking around the situation, market, wider environment and future possibilities;
- good communication engaging participation and interest;
- a sense of shared passion; and
- the flexibility to change the strategy when something new and important comes along

– and hard elements:

- data gathering and trend estimation;
- analysis of what is and what might be;
- 'what if' thinking and modelling;
- the numerical realities, possibilities and goals;

- the choices and exclusions required for proper focus; and
- the determination to make it stick

– but the process should be seamless and the balance fairly equal.

IDEAS, CREATIVITY AND THE CONSUMER

Although predominantly 'soft', ideas management often fails for lack of clear structure ('hard' elements):

- resource allocated to the endeavour;
- clear direction from a strategy or brief;
- techniques and structure to hold the activity and guide the creative(s); and
- clear, shared criteria for selection.

MANAGING PROJECTS

Projects need a good mix of head and heart. The soft elements would include:

- development of the idea or its execution, developmental consumer studies;
- the fit between the leader, the team and the task they face;
- how communication and teamwork is handled, especially between the team and the sponsors, stakeholders and the rest of the company; and
- individual and collective feelings about the project: enthusiasm, pride, doubts, etc.

Hard elements would include:

- the disciplines of project management – clear definition, planning and control;
- transparent risk management (not avoidance!);
- numerical analysis, evidence, data and proposals; and
- evaluative consumer/market research.

RESULTS AND LEARNING

Learning is also a mix. Typically the hard elements get most attention:

- post-launch evaluation about numbers and judgements of success; and
- documenting and filing the learning.

The numbers are important. They represent the reality of success and failure. However, it is often the soft elements that actually make learning stick:

- telling stories about the project;
- having a laugh about all the difficult moments and the fun;
- allowing proper anger and sadness if it went badly wrong;
- finding creative ways of communicating the learning;
- thinking about the audience; and
- finding the 'inlets'– the times people are receptive and need learning.

Since innovation demands varying combinations of the two worlds of creativity and judgement all the way through, much awareness and flexibility will be needed. Let us consider three ways of handling the difficulties both in terms of individual and organizational response.

- **Confusion** – not recognizing the two worlds.
- **Splitting** – trying to shut them off from each other.
- **Integration.**

THREE RESPONSES

1 CONFUSION

Trying to live in the two worlds of creativity and judgement at the same time can cause confusion. An example? Imagine a meeting at which investment decisions are being made on projects, decision papers have been submitted and the project leaders are attending the session in turns.

Several decisions have been made, including saying 'no' to one or two projects. Time is running out and the next meeting is about budget cuts. The atmosphere is one of pressure, focus and ruthlessness.

In walks one of the younger employees with a new idea. He has circulated a 'charter' asking for resources to explore an e-business that doesn't exactly fit the strategy but has intriguing elements and could be very promising.

Unless there is a switch into creative mode, the gatekeepers are going to say 'no'. At worst, their judgement will be a straight negative and the employee will leave thinking there is no interest in his idea. Slightly better would be a 'no' with some reasons attached; if the employee is really passionate about the idea, he will be able to do some more work. Better still: either the gatekeepers positively ask for more work to be done and give guidance, or they reschedule the item for another day when their minds aren't burdened by the cost-cutting meeting. Best of all, assuming the idea has real potential as well as rough edges, the meeting shifts gear into a brief creative session. Both the promising employee and the promising idea get inputs from the senior team and the result will be a good 'charter' with support in the business. An important by-product of this will be the increased understanding and confidence of the young employee.

In this example, what makes the difference is the flexibility of the senior team to move between the two worlds. Without it, confusion prevails. If an idea needing 'soft' handling lands in a 'hard' environment, a business opportunity may be lost.

2 SPLITTING

If the 'hard' and 'soft' thought worlds appear to be in conflict, it is tempting to split them apart so that they don't harm each other. As a result, we come to see them as separate and irreconcilable.

This split occurs in two ways.

● We categorize people as having more 'hard' or 'soft' characteristics, whether they are creative or good managers, etc.

● We reflect the split in the structure of the company.

Consciously or otherwise, people come to be labelled as either 'creative' or not. As a result, the two types can't understand each other and find it difficult to communicate. Another consequence is our attitude to creativity itself. Defining it in opposition to whatever is uncreative, we come to believe that creativity must be inherently undisciplined. Idea generation must have no boundaries, and it will be hampered by a brief; the creative people should have total freedom to pursue their imagination, unfettered by the demands of the business. The consequence for the business is poor management of the 'creative' functions. Research, product development or marketing may become a law unto themselves, lacking a clear focus or discipline for their work.

On the other hand, we may come to see judgement processes as inherently objective. Decisions are made with little or no regard for people's feelings, and communicated in a way that alienates and frustrates those involved. As a result, the business fails to develop a space where new ideas can be fostered, or management processes that adequately generate alternatives for consideration. Ideas wither and creativity dies off. The business atrophies.

Such splitting of mental functions, at its most extreme, doesn't work. It damages people and organizations and threatens the innovation process. So why does it happen?

Psychoanalyst Melanie Klein describes splitting as a basic psychological defence motivated by fear. The term is used extensively to describe mental processes whereby we ease life's complexity by splitting the good from the bad. According to Klein, we all have the ability and the need, from time to time, to do this.

Splitting, says Klein, derives from a time when as a baby we didn't yet know that others are separate beings. In order to cope with overwhelming feelings (rage, fear and so on – which all infants are subject to), we project them out onto the other person (mother). This means mother temporarily becomes a terrifying witch, all badness. If the infant is lucky, mother understands and can be robust and empathetic. She bears his pain and her own which is invoked by empathy. She processes and understands these feelings for him until he can slowly realize and take back what is his, and become his own person. He can then see both good and bad, but the capacity to split remains with him and is employed again in certain situations.

Splitting may occur because of fears that one thing will damage another. The baby fears that his rage and hate will destroy his love for his mother; he must therefore disown it. In the case of innovation, we fear that one element will destroy the other: that the creative people will be 'tainted' by participating in business judgement and discipline, that judges will 'go soft' if asked to have ideas. Mental boundaries are then constructed to split creativity and judgement.

There are occasions when mild splitting is necessary. Think of the marketing/advertising agency relationship, where much of this specialist creativity does reside in one side. But then the relationship is sometimes difficult, and maintaining the connections – one side understanding and trusting the other, information flowing freely between people – is of paramount importance. Total splitting won't do the job.

3 INTEGRATION

What is integration? If it is neither confusion nor splitting, then what is it? What does it 'feel' like?

In business, some individuals and groups *do* seem to be able to manage different situations more flexibly than others. Understanding and valuing difference seems to be one of the great challenges of being human. To live happily and productively, we need to come to terms with difference, and to value others who have what we have not. We need to accept envy.

Envy is tough. Nobody wants to be seen as envious; relatively few people are able to acknowledge that they are somehow less than other people. Envy is a state of belittlement that most of us cannot endure for long. We employ an array of mental defences to avoid it. However, some of us may be able to endure the thought for long enough to recover a lost part of ourselves; the tiny, totally dependent and powerless infant who fears being overcome.

I think it is important to see integration as a continuing process rather than a 'fix'. It means knowing our shadow side as well as the side that is in the light. Knowing ourselves isn't comfortable, but it enables us to separate ourselves truly from others. We no longer need to project onto others those parts of ourselves and feelings we find unacceptable; our relationships become more productive.

Integration means becoming a whole person, rather than a collection of strengths and weaknesses. It's a tough call.

FOUR TOUGH CHALLENGES

When we value difference, we can explore and exploit the two worlds of creativity and judgement more fully. We can create more fully and judge where to spend resources more soundly. Here are four points at which the issues of integration and understanding of the two worlds might be most important.

1 **Objectivity.** Gatekeepers need to achieve real objectivity in their decisions while knowing about the soft issues and planning to deal with them.
2 **Expectations.** The gap between the project team and the business sponsors or gatekeepers needs to be well managed.
3 **Actually doing the strategy.** We need to incorporate strategy into the management processes, and not leave it as a thinking process disconnected from business reality.
4 **Letting new ideas live.** We need to find successful ways of nurturing ideas that aren't yet fully grown.

OBJECTIVE GATEKEEPING
Decision making is fundamentally about being good at the hard stuff. Paradoxically, however, it is the failure to manage soft issues that most

often gets in the way of objectivity. Here are just a few of the possible distractions.

- **We don't want to disappoint the team.** The project team has put so much effort into the project and is keen for its success.
- **We don't want to unsettle them.** If we stop this project, what are they going to do next? They might leave before we can sort out their next assignment.
- **We have to do something!** Sales managers desperately need activity to appease customers in a competitive or declining market. Where is the activity for next autumn?
- **If we don't do it now...** Restructuring is around the corner. The decision to launch this project may well get taken out of our hands if we don't decide quickly.
- **Marketing are the experts, aren't they?** Marketing thinking isn't challenged or marketing people reject challenge; it 'isn't done' or there is fear of offending the marketing team. After all, they are the experts, aren't they?
- **Collective optimism.** This is 'groupthink'. Because a group likes innovation and wants it to work, they stop seeing the negatives. Positive thinking at all times becomes an unwritten rule. An influential leader can sometimes persuade a group into this mode, or the company culture can be insufficiently critical of innovation.
- **Selective perception.** 'There are lies, damned lies and statistics.' Any consumer research will have some measures which look better than others. If only the good numbers get presented, then objectivity is put in doubt.
- **Fear of evidence.** 'Market research kills ideas', say some. This is back to splitting! Sometimes there is a management culture that says real men don't need research – instinct is what matters.
- **Box-ticking.** The team stops thinking and puts answers in boxes without really knowing why. They assume that the system will make the decision for them. They fail to declare any feelings or strong recommendation, leaving the responsibility to the gatekeepers.

- **Desire for certainty.** It is human to want more proof, but we need to weigh up what is more valuable, speed or certainty. Sir John Harvey-Jones once said that if you are absolutely certain about a decision, then you can also be sure that you are too late! In my company, we have rushed into bad decisions having falsely persuaded ourselves that the competition were hot on our heels.
- **The funnel is full already.** If we accept this project, we may have to stop doing something else, which can cause pain and disappointment.
- **Project chameleon.** The project has changed but the gatekeepers aren't fully aware. They don't fully understand or recognize the decision being proposed.
- **Strategy shift.** The strategy is changing and the team isn't fully aware. The project is no longer appropriate and should really be stopped, but it isn't the team's fault and the gatekeepers for various reasons don't want to reveal all just now.
- **What exactly are we here to decide?** The decision paper is either poor or too late to be read in advance. Nobody is really clear what the decision is. Worse: the team or the gatekeepers thought it was time for a 'gate' and are presenting a review, not a decision. A review might be perfectly appropriate, but it needs a different mental space and preparation.
- **Time, ladies and gentlemen.** Maybe the gatekeepers are being presented with too many small decisions; maybe they are delegating too little. Maybe they haven't allocated enough time. Important discussions on major decisions are rushed.

All of these dilemmas can assail the gatekeepers as they strive to make wise and innovative decisions. The overall effect may be a bias towards leniency and low hurdles, or it may be the other way – insufficient vision. It is vital that gatekeepers are aware of the forces operating on them so that these can be accounted for and then countered or put aside.

Here are a few guidelines to help gatekeepers achieve this difficult goal.

- **Separate and take responsibility for the people issues.** Encourage the team to articulate feelings and take them into account. Sometimes feelings are the tip of an iceberg; there is a reason beneath them waiting to be understood.
- **Reward teams for sensible 'stop' decisions.** They are saving precious resource and are rarely recognized for difficult decisions of this kind. The money saved on good 'stops' can be significant.
- **Know your track record.** Is your business habitually over-cautious, launching too little or too late? Is it over-optimistic and under-critical? What is the proportion of innovation failures to innovation successes? Add up the launch proposals and publish an analysis. If senior management show an ability to face up to mistakes, others will learn this important skill too.
- **Know each other.** Acknowledge diverse skills in the gatekeeping team. Use your optimists and realists effectively. If you have any paragons of objectivity in your organization, consider recruiting them to the gatekeeping team.
- **Demand evidence and 'gut feeling' in equal measure.** Consider training your gatekeepers in cognitive decision-making and thinking techniques.
- **Encourage challenge.** Gatekeepers must take the lead here. This is good for the culture and the project. If they don't encourage challenge, gatekeeping meetings will be sterile, obedient affairs.
- **Manage the flow of projects.** Strategy means choosing what *not* to do as well as what to do. If the funnel is empty, direct resources towards idea generation on an important area of the strategy. If the funnel is too full, you must get tough: check the benefits and risks of new and old projects against your strategy and winnow accordingly.
- **Make the strategy public.** Keep publishing the strategy and reminding people of the goals and values of the organization.

Gatekeeping is time-consuming and the decision makers are often very busy people.

BECOMING A BETTER GATEKEEPER

✓ Be realistic about the gatekeeping agenda.

✓ Ask for – and read – project documents in good time.

✓ Settle any single-function issues before the gatekeeping meeting.

✓ Manage time in the meeting itself.

✓ If you feel that you are rushing decisions, allocate more time.

✓ If necessary, take smaller decisions elsewhere so the gatekeeping team concentrates on the big ones.

NEGOTIATING EXPECTATIONS – THE GAP BETWEEN THE TEAM AND THE BUSINESS

Project teams and gatekeepers rarely meet to negotiate expectations. A conflict of expectations tabled at the *start* of the project can be a very creative beginning, but a conflict that surfaces later can cause damage. Projects generate stress, which needs to be balanced with a sense of progress. When progress is lacking or stalled, the stress is more likely to be converted to blaming and negative behaviour, and the conflict will be much harder to resolve. Every project has to balance cost, time and performance. Gatekeepers must establish their expectations in these areas. If they don't, the project team may set their own expectations and deliver a result that over-delivers in some areas and under-delivers in others. Teams, on the other hand, must raise issues as they emerge; gatekeepers can't be as close to the work.

Gatekeepers need to ask for options in terms of time, performance and cost, and not simply issue deadlines. For example, if a team thinks that time is the top priority, they will act accordingly, taking more risks with performance and cost. Gatekeepers may suddenly find the budget over-spent or performance figures unavailable because of lack of testing time! They must ask: What will performance look like if the time target is to be achieved? Can the budget go up to buy more resource? How long would the project take if the desired tests are all done? Then options can be generated and choices made that best suit the situation.

TRADING EXPECTATIONS – THE TRIPLE CONSTRAINT

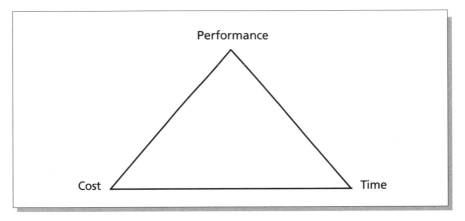

Here are some typical questions that the gatekeepers will need to ask to help establish the right balance.

Performance
- Are there competitive benchmarks or customer expectations we must meet? How important are they?
- Are we bound by legal or regulatory standards and are they negotiable?
- Can we drop any standards of performance?
- What happens to time and cost when we change performance standards?

Time
- How likely is it that there is a competitor hot on our heels?
- What is the expected timescale?
- What delays, risks and dilemmas can we foresee?
- Will delay affect other projects?
- If the project starts to slip, how will we know?
- Can the team reduce slippage without extra resource?

- Will performance improve if we add time?
- Can the customer accept delay?
- Can we re-schedule?
- Can we quantify time changes in terms of cost?

Cost
- Is there a budget?
- Do we understand the major costs?
- Are there issues of viability/payback? Are there some definite cost boundaries?
- How can we reduce product/service cost?
- Should we do it now or save cost reduction measures until phase 2?
- Would the customer accept any extra cost?
- Can we offer new benefits in return for extra cost?
- Can we absorb any extra cost?

Two points are so important that they almost go without saying. First, projects have different requirements and priorities and nothing will be achieved by trying to nail down all three corners at the outset; flexibility will be needed to accommodate new information. Secondly, the conversation about expectations should expand to include every aspect of the project. It should be continuous and explicit. The price of stalling the conversation is high.

The negotiation begins by clarifying the project's purpose. What is this task? What would success look like? Is everybody clear where the stretch is and where the big resource demands will be? Roles and responsibilities need to be defined, and people found to fit them, especially the best leader for the job. The sponsor and gatekeeper roles must also be negotiated and understood.

There will always be a gap somewhere between the needs of the project and the current capabilities of the people. All learning solutions should

THE NEGOTIATION PROCESS

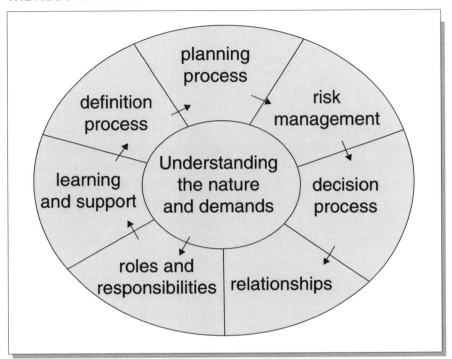

be considered: training, workshops, mentoring from 'old hands', gathering wisdom from previous projects, relevant external case studies.

Sponsors and gatekeepers, too, should consider their contribution, their suitability for the task, and the possible sources of help and inspiration for them.

Defining the project is particularly important when an organization runs different kinds of projects.

The project team and sponsors should ask:

- Who has a say in defining the project?
- What is the outcome we really need to achieve in the long term?
- Who needs to know the definition?

The project definition in turn should lead to a thorough planning process that includes thinking about risk and about who will be responsible for decision making. This is the time to get real about the triple constraint (performance/time/cost).

Finally, relationships are rarely negotiated. The question 'How would we like it to be round here?' is sometimes asked inside the project team but rarely gets shared with the gatekeepers, despite what is at stake. Projects generate uncertainty, risk and pressure; team and gatekeepers must enjoy an open and trusting relationship to manage the risks well.

Everything here involves the mixture of hard and soft elements that we have explored so far. If teams and gatekeepers can attend to both the hard skills of project and risk management, and the soft skills of relationships, feelings, expectations and creativity, then innovation projects will have a far better chance of succeeding.

STRATEGY INTO ACTION – THINKING AND DOING

Strategies can come under pressure because short-term targets take precedence over longer-term strategic goals. When this happens repeatedly, people may feel that strategy is merely a thinking exercise, and not 'real'.

This frustration must be dealt with. It won't go away, but the balance can be improved by keeping the horizon in view. It should be part of the company's portfolio management routine – or part of a balanced scorecard approach – to keep the strategy alive by checking progress, and to provide some quantification of any change in resource allocation. If we pull back or reduce a launch in order to cut marketing spend and hit a short-term target, we should be conscious of the effect on long-term growth, and not pretend the gap will be made up by magic.

Let me expand on one mechanism for charting progress. When the analysis is done, the choices made and the goals set for the longer term, strategy can then consist of two main dimensions. One of these is qualitative:

- the overall direction desired;
- definition of priority and non-priority areas;

- ideally some outline thoughts about how to tackle the core areas and what it is that the company can uniquely offer.

The other is quantitative:

- rough quantification of where the business might go if nothing new is undertaken (market share, turnover, growth, profit) – called the 'ongoing business';
- a statement of intent as to where the business wants to be, what would constitute success, expressed as quantitative goals (share, turnover, growth, profit);
- allowing a simple calculation of the gap between the ongoing business model and the required growth, ie the 'innovation gap'.

FRAMEWORK DEVELOPED BY PROFESSOR HAX AT HARVARD

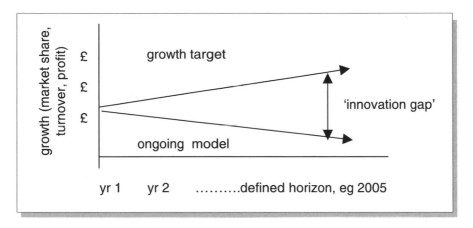

For tracking progress, I want to focus on a method that mimics and balances the 'gap-filling' instinct we rely on to manage shorter-term targets. (We check to see if we are on plan; if we aren't, we identify the size of the gap and then seek to fill it.)

This method requires a number of disciplines that may be new.

- **Strategy must have this quantitative element.** Aspirations must be converted into numbers, with an understanding that the accuracy of the long term is quite different to the here and now of this year's profit. It is like another language.

● **Projects must make some estimates out to the year of the strategic horizon.** This will present difficulties in the early stages of definition and development, and judgements will have to be made about where in the life of a project it becomes reasonable to ask for numbers.

● **Adding up the project numbers must include an allowance for the likelihood of success.** Historic performance is the only realistic guide. This 'aiming off' must happen at the portfolio level only, so that individual projects can plan for success.

● **The definition of the word 'project' may need to be re-negotiated** to include all major activities contributing to the 'innovation gap', if the existing definition is narrower.

PROJECT PORTFOLIO VALUE VS 'INNOVATION GAP'

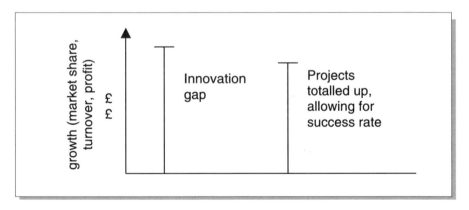

Once we accept these ideas, at least experimentally, we can compare the expected value of the project portfolio with the innovation gap, and by implication the strategic goals. We can review resource allocation if the results look unexciting, either to expand the most promising initiatives and get more out of them, or to stop the less beneficial projects in favour of a well briefed search for new ideas. If the numbers simply won't add up, then we need to discuss how realistic the strategic goals are, and how important it is to raise the success rate of projects.

NURTURING NEW IDEAS

This last challenge is not the least. I want to talk about a particular stage in idea generation, not about the whole landscape between the call for ideas and the start of projects.

First, idea generation is not a homogenous process. Hypothesizing about consumer need is different from gathering raw ideas; brainstorming is different from building and nurturing ideas, and from polishing concepts.

Although idea generation is slightly different each time, below is a typical route-map for an idea generation exercise.

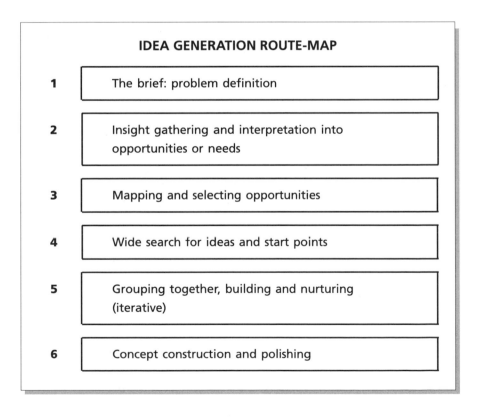

IDEA GENERATION ROUTE-MAP

1 The brief: problem definition

2 Insight gathering and interpretation into opportunities or needs

3 Mapping and selecting opportunities

4 Wide search for ideas and start points

5 Grouping together, building and nurturing (iterative)

6 Concept construction and polishing

The most difficult stage is the fifth – the selection, building and nurturing of ideas. However well thought out the brief, however insightful the hypotheses about consumer need, however energetic the brainstorming of raw ideas, the crunch comes when half-formed ideas have to be sifted and chosen for further building, or left behind. The difficulty is telling the flowers from the weeds, at a stage when they all tend to look the same. It is at this stage that premature judgement can kill the most novel ideas, and ideas and their creators are most sensitive to management behaviour.

I witnessed an example at the beginning of my career when managers at Brooke Bond were looking for new ideas about tea. They had a very successful business in the early 1980s and no urgent need to innovate. When the idea came along for round teabags, we subjected it to the usual scrutiny, in this case with explorative discussion groups. When groups of consumers informed us that a mere gimmick such as a new shape wouldn't influence their purchasing, we took their remarks at face value. After some debate, we dropped the idea. Our competitor took an entirely different view and complemented their qualitative research with a quantitative approach, assessing consumers' likelihood to purchase in a more realistic setting and not asking them for justification in front of their peers. It resulted a few years later in Tetley's very successful launch of the round teabag. Of course, there was later a happy ending for Unilever, when we retaliated with the pyramid bag (which I am proud to have been associated with), but not before many unhappy market share charts and profit revisions underlined the lesson: good ideas can die easily.

The key mistake with round teabags was the poor use and interpretation of consumer research. More often, the novel idea is lost because internal judgements and criticism (numbers, attempts to over-rationalize, statements about priority, analysis and criticism) don't help the idea to develop. Strong creators may help the idea to survive, but it can get a rough ride.

Fragile new ideas must be nurtured. Every new idea, as someone once said, is born drowning. Gatekeepers need deliberately to seek out the kernel and the promise of the idea, no matter what deficiencies it has.

Nurturing can be difficult. If it's not valued in an organization, people don't practise and it fails to become part of the culture. If a company spends most of its time trying to improve efficiency – or fight fires – then the behaviour that wins recognition will tend to be the critical, judgmental behaviour that is good for identifying negatives.

Also, envy may rear its head. It takes humility to value someone else's idea when it's different from ours; to value it when raw and unfinished takes us right back to the moments when we presented our first creative efforts to adults. We are being asked to empathize with the idea creator and to bear with them the fragile state of the infant, so to speak.

If our own first efforts got little encouragement, we will have a greater burden of envy to bear when asked to support someone else's creativity.

The nurturing phase – language, values, behaviours
So, we need a culture for supporting ideas at the moment when they most need it, and recognizing that moment when it arrives.

The guiding principle in this phase is that we are seeking to understand an idea, rather than to judge it. We must 'find the magic'. How might we do this?

- Create space for the idea.
- Give it attention.
- Seek to make it real by visualizing, demonstrating and making prototypes.
- Ask first what is good about the idea, not what is wrong.
- Build on ideas and invite others to build and transform our own.
- Keep judgement at bay (avoiding critical questions, comparisons, numerical analysis or evaluation) just for a while.
- Allow our intuition to speak: patiently wait for our instincts to emerge.

It helps to establish a shared language of idea nurture. If the team can negotiate a set of terms that everybody recognizes and uses, the necessary values and behaviours come more easily.

Let me offer you the language, values and behaviours developed in our marketing and development departments at Van den Bergh. They have been discussed and developed by the team as a whole, and we find them particularly useful in the nurturing phase, when we are trying to help ideas survive rather than killing them off.

LANGUAGE, VALUES, BEHAVIOURS – VAN DEN BERGH

- Vision: 'Growing me, growing you, aha!'
- Values:
  – feeling, supporting, connecting, 'I will', excelling.
- Behaviours:
  – raging curiosity
  – finding the magic
  – bravery
  – time-lording
  – making it real
  – signalling
  – 'I will'.

'Growing me, growing you, aha!' stands as a kind of motto for the whole stack of principles. It sounds a little silly – and perhaps it is; we needed to loosen up. It makes a connection between business growth and our own personal growth and unpacks into five values:

- bringing our feelings to work;
- being able to support others;
- connecting to the outside world;
- the idea that 'I will' do something and not just complain from the sidelines; and
- the idea that we desire excellence, not making do with the merely adequate.

We have also identified a number of behaviours that we seek to use at work.

- **'Raging curiosity'** means going out and finding out, constantly looking for stimulus from the outside world.
- **'Finding the magic'** is a reminder to start with the positive, to learn to look for the core goodness inside an idea first.
- **'Bravery'** is not tolerating obstacles; finding the courage to speak out and challenge the politics, the negative feelings and the processes that may be blocking ideas.
- **'Time-lording'** is the collective responsibility for time. It is about the way we consciously and unconsciously choose to spend that precious resource, and work towards more intelligent choices.
- **'Making it real'** says that ideas live when we get them out of our heads, out of the purely verbal and into as many of the senses as possible. Visualizing, prototyping and enacting all help to make ideas real for others.
- **'Signalling'** is about announcing the way we are thinking, so that we can distinguish 'hard' from 'soft' and use each as appropriate, especially when we are together in meetings. It also means giving things a context, whether that is a business context or a personal context. If we respond negatively to an idea because we have just had some personal bad news, it is best to signal this so that the other person knows.
- **'I will'** is a promise to be proactive; to engage in action rather than comment, to play on the pitch rather than judge from the stands.

If you spoke to anybody in our department and asked about these values, I think they'd be able to recreate them pretty accurately. They form a common language, and a common approach, which makes it easier for ideas to flourish. We are trying to identify and contain the hard elements of judgement and criticism so that they can't undermine creativity.

The difficulty may be illustrated by one last example. This story comes from a company with a good reputation for creativity, Hewlett Packard (HP), and it goes roughly like this... An employee notices that one of the company's technologies could be used in a novel way for a new product outside the company's existing range. After some early work to shape the idea, he presents it to his seniors. He is told that this is very creative but not an area of interest for HP. The employee is undaunted and does more. A second more defined presentation goes down badly and he is told to concentrate on other things.

I don't know how many iterations of this there are, but it is said that, after some considerable period of working on the idea in his spare time, the intrepid soul tries again and at last gets a better reception. Later, at the launch, when the product is clearly destined to provide HP with an important and profitable new line of business, Dave Packard himself goes to the man's office with a medal that he presents 'for persistence and obstinacy far beyond the call of engineering duty'!

Cycles of innovation

KEVIN BYRON

Kevin Byron received his doctorate in applied physics at the University of Hull in 1974. He then joined Nortel Networks' Harlow Laboratories (formerly Standard Telecommunication Laboratory) in the UK, where he was engaged in research into lasers and optical telecommunications technology. He is currently Manager of Technology at Harlow and has recently developed workshops on creativity and inventiveness.

Innovation is often seen as essentially a uni-directional process that begins with an idea and ends with a product. The development stages in this process have typically been characterized by a tilted S-shaped curve (see overleaf), where the vertical axis represents a value proposition, expressed either in technological or economic terms, and the horizontal axis is effort applied. This axis is often labelled 'time' but this is based on the false assumption that time alone is a measure of progress.

The tilted S-curve has three stages: a relatively slow research and development period, followed by rapid growth as the product/technology finds widespread application, and then maturity when the technology becomes self-limited. This curve gives a reasonably accurate picture of progress within a technology and is one that has been used in forecasting. However, when we examine the actual experience of teams of people working on technology innovation, far from perceiving such a neat progression from beginning to end, the innovation curve is more complex.

Over a longer timescale, there is an overall cyclicity in the activity focused on innovation. More specifically, once a technology has reached maturity, the same questions and challenges that arose from the original vision that gave birth to it are often asked again and a new cycle of innovation is embarked upon. The cycle of innovation can be re-started repeatedly and progress can continue unhindered provided the limits at the top of the S-curve are technological rather than physical.

CLASSIC S-SHAPED GROWTH CURVE

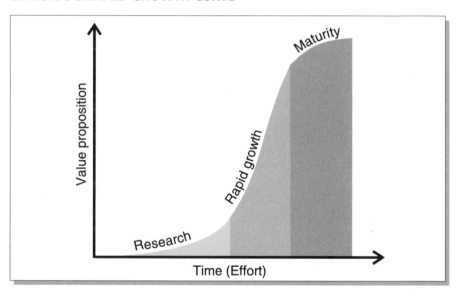

The first stage of this curve is motivated by the original vision which, after a protracted period of research and development effort, results in pre-production prototypes of the new technology, whether they be components, modules or complete systems. Here, the technological advantage is only being realized gradually because progress is punctuated by the many issues and challenges that need to be overcome before the product is successfully developed. Again, although this is shown as a smooth curve, a more detailed and expanded view of the progress during this period would reveal several discontinuities as both breakthroughs and setbacks in progress arise. The curve would also reveal smaller cycles that connect back to ideas that proved impractical earlier on but now, with the benefit of new knowledge, provide real value to the emerging technology or product.

Another discontinuity that can occur on this curve is due to 'disruptive technologies'. These are technologies that bring a different value proposition to the one currently being pursued and are generally successful in another smaller market segment alongside the one they ultimately disrupt. When their true potential is realized, they migrate to the larger market and overtake the existing technology or product.

Product development times across many markets are currently anything up to three years years, whereas 20 years ago they were often as long as 15-20 years. So for businesses which are competing in rapidly evolving marketplaces such as telecommunications, innovation management based on practical experience of what happens and what could happen during the development of a technology is essential. This is as important in research as it is in product development, though it is only relatively recently, with the much tighter coupling of these activities, that models of innovation management in research have been developed.

Let us consider the experience of a real world laboratory: Nortel Networks' Harlow Laboratories.

THE HARLOW LABORATORIES

The Harlow Laboratories are Nortel Networks' largest in Europe and have a proud history of original thinking and breakthrough innovation that has been responsible for some of the founding technological milestones of modern telecommunications.

- Alex Reeves invented Pulse Code Modulation (PCM) in 1937. This method for converting analogue signals, such as speech or video, into a digital format ready for transmission is an underpinning technology for today's digital world.
- Charles Kao and George Hockham launched the optical communication revolution in 1966 with the publication of the first paper propos-

ing optical fibre and laser light as a viable telecommunications medium. The pioneering work that continues at Harlow establishes Nortel Networks as a true world leader in this exciting field.

- In the 1970s, engineers at Harlow created the first radio on a single semiconductor chip, opening the way for the era of advanced wireless mobile communication.

This tradition of innovation continues to the present day and engineers at Harlow file well over 150 new invention studies or patents each year.

One of the key strengths of the Harlow Laboratories is the co-location of technology and product development teams. Methodologies are shared more easily and concepts are able to migrate across traditional boundaries more readily, and so spark new ideas. The speed with which leading edge technology can be incorporated at each stage of a product's development drives differentiation and keeps Nortel Networks' solutions ahead of the competition.

Research and development at the Harlow Labs can be categorized (see Technology vs Product Matrix diagram opposite) across various levels of maturity ranging from 'product-ready' through 'evolving' to 'stretch' technology (technology that extends to physically realizable limits) and, ultimately, to the aforementioned 'disruptive' technology.

Products arising at these various levels of technology maturity range from those currently under development and undergoing further improvement through to 'next generation' products and beyond to radically new products. Development teams working on current and improved products focus on cost reduction and feature addition, and this can span the technology maturity space almost up to the boundary of disruptive technology. Teams working on next generation products are principally involved with emerging technologies that stretch the limits of existing technology and bring on-line new technologies that are emerging from the research stage.

In the disruptive technology space, which is high risk but has potentially high returns on investment, activity is focused on predicting the trajectory of technologies that are not in the immediate field of view. This

TECHNOLOGY VS PRODUCT MATRIX

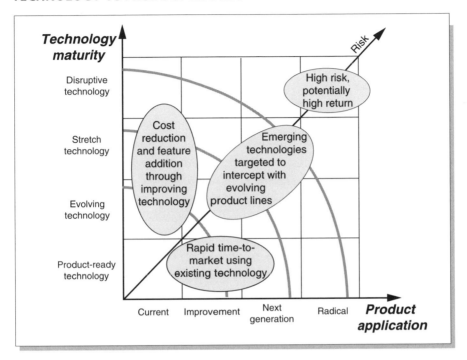

activity also includes working with, and supporting, university research in the UK and Europe and involvement in EU and UK government sponsored collaborative projects with other industries and universities.

The work at Harlow is of strategic importance, not just to Nortel Networks but to the industry as a whole. The engineers are helping carriers to evolve their networks to support the growing demand for exciting new services such as interactive multimedia, video and high-speed internet access. Teams at Harlow are involved in just about every aspect of network design, development and usage, from components through to system architectures and applications. Every project draws on the rich diversity of talents, skills and technical know-how of the engineers to ensure that Nortel Networks' solutions are market leaders.

With rapidly developing telecommunications markets, Harlow Labs have sustained their activity across all of these areas of technology maturity and product development and this again is reflected in the high output of creativity in terms of new products, new product concepts and intellectual property.

PRODUCT DEVELOPMENT MODELS

Different standard models have been adopted and adapted over recent years by a number of industries since product development was first identified as a process. Three examples that have been used in the telecommunications industry are briefly reviewed below. This summary is by no means comprehensive; it merely thumbnails some of the changes in product development processes that have been created to keep pace with the dramatic changes that have taken place in this business.

In common with many industries, these changes have been driven by globalization, which in turn has been partly enabled by global deregulation in the business. On a technical level, the market has been driven by an unprecedented demand for bandwidth, precipitated by the expansion of the internet, e-business and e-commerce and by a parallel expansion in mobile communication.

One of the earlier product development models was known as the 'Gate Process'. This saw product development as a linear process divided into phases, from definition through design, development and trials to release and on-going support. A gate is a milestone and a management checkpoint where formal approval is sought.

To proceed from one phase to the next, passage through a gate is required and this is achieved by a meeting with representatives from the various teams involved in the development of the product. At this meeting, the state of development of the product is assessed against a number of criteria. These criteria typically include the appropriateness of the technology, the degree of customer engagement, the state of the business plan, and so on. If all criteria are met satisfactorily, the next stage of development ensues.

The Gate Process as originally defined worked well, but as product development times shrank three key limiting factors became apparent.

- The Gate Process was too slow and risk-averse. It did not have the facility for getting ahead by overlapping adjacent stages.
- The customer was not engaged early enough. As a result, the development of the product could diverge from what the customer actually wanted.
- Different teams tended to be involved at different stages of the process. Few people saw the development of a product through from start to finish.

In many cases, it was not necessary to discard the Gate Process but modify it in order to adapt to the changing circumstances of product development. However, it was largely superseded by a new process that was better matched to the changing business environment.

Known as 'Alpha/Beta Ship', this process sought to overcome the limitations of the Gate Process, in the first instance by reducing the number of phases to make the process quicker. Secondly, more emphasis was put on customer engagement from the very start. Finally, one team was identified to see the process through from start to finish.

This new process has the advantage of a degree of iterative flexibility that is a closer match to the cyclical nature of innovation. The process begins with dialogue to establish the customer's needs, followed by an alpha phase in which the product is designed and built to those bare specifications. Further engagement with the customer leads iteratively through a series of improvements and modifications to a beta phase, in which the product is released – perhaps several times – with increased functionality and higher quality. Finally, the product is shipped to the customer.

So the Alpha/Beta Ship model eliminated some of the gates, resulting in a more efficient process that involved one product development team and engaged the customer more fully.

More recently, the model sometimes known as 'Time To Market' (TTM) for product development has gained in popularity in many companies.

This model is shown below as a funnelled pipeline through which products flow. At the input end, there are lots of potential product ideas; at the output just a few successful ones emerge that have a high chance of success. Along the pipeline, there are various points where business decisions are made to filter out the more speculative product ideas as early as possible. This also allows maximum resource and velocity to be applied to the winners. To enable this filtering, a structured development process is set in place to provide an effective dialogue between the technical and the marketing experts. In a sense, the tapered pipeline symbolizes the tighter interaction required between these two disciplines as the new product opportunities are identified. These experts are organized into two teams: an inter-disciplinary portfolio management team, drawn from marketing, general managers and technical experts, and an integrated project team that is responsible for each of the successful products that make it through the pipeline.

TTM PRODUCT PIPELINE

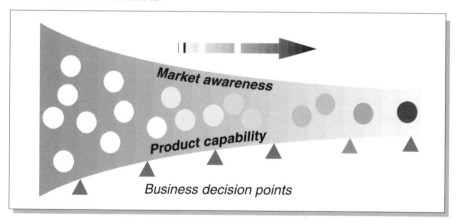

AN INNOVATION MODEL FOR RESEARCH

These product development models are appropriate to product development and manufacture. However, given the much tighter coupling that now exists between research and product development, it became necessary to develop a process model for mapping the route from invention to innovation. This model deals with the earlier stages of product development: in the TTM model described earlier, the stages that lead up to the input to the product development funnel. These stages involve research, idea generation and a methodology for identifying the ideas that can win through to the product pipeline.

At Harlow Labs, an adaptation of the TTM pipeline model has been adopted for this purpose. This model again can be visualized (see below) as one or more funnelled pipelines, known as technology pipelines, which interface to the input of the product pipeline. ('IPR' in the diagram stands for intellectual property rights.)

A TTM MODEL FOR RESEARCH AND PRODUCT DEVELOPMENT

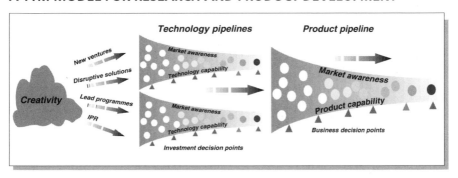

At the front of the technology pipeline ideas are generated. No process can be assigned to the inventiveness needed for new idea generation, but putting in place the right environment is essential for nurturing creativity. At Harlow Labs, this environment has been created around the organization of multi-disciplinary teams, good interaction with marketing experts to identify discontinuities in the market, broad involvement in university research, a reward scheme for innovative ideas and a modern, well-equipped environment in which to work.

In this innovation process model, new ideas are reviewed by a technology taskforce and the outcomes from this review include new ventures, lead programmes, disruptive solutions and intellectual property rights. The new ventures and lead programmes are incorporated into technology proposals that feed into the TTM process proper. These are reviewed at investment decision points along the technology pipeline, with progress according to investment need, function, performance and cost. The two linked pipelines (technology and product) in this model differ primarily in the length of the pipeline. Product development typically takes longer; the technology investment process might be compressed into a few months or even weeks. Other important features of the technology pipeline are that there is minimal procedural interference to ensure that creativity can flow, there is no pre-determined product alignment in the early stages and there is scope for the re-use of ideas in other contexts, and also the re-cycling of ideas. The recycling of ideas is essential in the technology pipeline because many ideas have their own timing. Provision needs to be built into the process to bring them forward at the appropriate stage.

CYCLES OF INNOVATION

As well as those teams involved in research leading to new product introductions which work with the TTM model for innovation or local variants on it, there are also teams focused on developing the future strategy for the various technologies. This requires a wider perspective on the process methodologies looking over a longer time frame, and it is here that one can discern a cyclical pattern in innovation.

The cycle shown in the diagram opposite starts with market and technology awareness. Customers are engaged and their requirements identified. From this awareness, the engineers develop innovative concepts and secure the intellectual property rights for their ideas. They next design the system and this provides a vision of how they can make the innovation happen. Then comes value assessment again, with close engagement with the customer even before any products are developed. Value assessment creates the demand for new technology and innovation to meet that demand. At this stage, another dialogue takes place, this time with the bodies that set industry standards. None of this technology can be developed in isolation from standards bodies. In many industries – and in telecommunications in particular – it is essential to work with the standards bodies to ensure that new innovations will fit with existing technologies. This interaction actually creates a feedback loop. The standards bodies may not allow an industry to do everything they want, so this means going back to the customer with revised requirements and engaging in the value assessment again. The wider cycle then moves from the technological innovation through to de-risk, where safety and feasibility are built into the technology. The outcome of this completes the cycle with the creation of a new capability, out of which comes new products. The whole process now starts again when new opportunities are identified through further dialogue with the customers using the new technology. Rather than a purely circular process, it is perhaps more accurately described as an outward spiral, in that each new cycle extends the boundaries of the previous capability.

SCHEMATIC OF AN INNOVATION CYCLE IN TELECOMMUNICATIONS

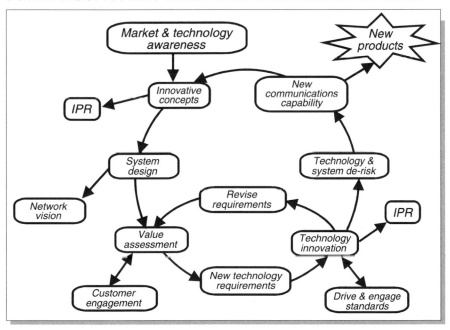

An illustration of the cyclical nature of innovation can clearly be seen in the various generations of optical fibre communication for the long haul market. By the mid-1980s, the market for optical communication was well established and fibre-based communication systems underwent widespread deployment. Since that time to the present day, a number of generations of optical communication system have come and gone, and the end of each generation was marked by a challenge to overcome the limitations on information throughput.

As the cycle of each generation was completed, the same question was being asked by the engineers who design the systems. This question, in its simplest form, asked how an even greater transmission capacity could be achieved that would also be economically viable and bring greater value to customers.

The design of each new generation of fibre system represented a new capability that had overcome the limitations to transmission capacity of the previous generation. These limitations were due to dispersion, sometimes known as pulse spreading in the fibre or losses in the fibre, though other limitations have appeared in the most recent generation of system. Dispersion and loss limited the information-carrying capacity of an optical fibre in the earlier generations of this technology. For example, one generation of fibre in the late 1980s, which used laser sources emitting at 1.3uM, was limited in its throughput by the losses at that wavelength. By shifting the wavelength out to 1.55uM, where the losses were lower, a greater throughput was achieved.

The development of optical amplifiers at that wavelength in the late 1990s meant that dispersion now became the dominant limiting factor, though another limitation known as non-linearity also appeared, when high bit-rate, multi-wavelength systems were developed (technically known as 'Dense Wavelength Division Multiplexed' systems). So, although new problems emerged as bandwidth capability grew from 10s of MBit/sec in the 1980s to 1,000s of GBit/Sec in the 1990s, the challenges for greater capacity that drove the cycle of innovation remained fundamentally the same.

Clearly these cycles cannot go on interminably and eventually technological limitations come up against physical limitations. Before this stage is reached, however, there is real value for the teams working on future innovation strategy in recognizing these cycles and where any particular technology is on the cycle. This wider time perspective has other benefits, in that ideas and technologies that may have been discarded in one cycle of innovation may become critically important in a subsequent cycle. An example of this in the world of optical communication is Raman fibre amplifiers. Research on Raman amplifiers was carried out by labs worldwide in the mid-1980s but, before reaching the product development phase, it was superseded by a more efficient amplifier based on erbium-doped fibre. However, Raman amplifiers returned to disrupt some segments of the amplifier market in a subsequent innovation cycle, when the unique advantages that it offered could be fully exploited.

Interestingly, it was developments in the competing fibre amplifier technology that re-vitalized research on the Raman amplifier. This has the hallmarks of a disruptive technology, but the important difference is that the Raman fibre amplifier did not reach the product stage in a niche market at the time of its earlier development. So, perhaps more accurately, it could be defined as 'disruptive research'. The importance in examples like this of the bigger picture of innovation cycles is in securing intellectual property rights early in the development of new technologies, and also maintaining a certain level of know-how in these areas. The challenge, of course, is in backing the winners amongst the many potential areas of research that can be pursued, which highlights the importance of having an effective innovation process model.

Predicting the future, however, can never be an exact science since discovery is completely unpredictable. Nevertheless, applying a certain level of 'process' that combines the TTM model of innovation with the cycles of innovation perspective can provide some useful insights into the future evolution of technology.

CONCLUSIONS

In the highly competitive world of technology innovation, engineers are working in product development cycles that are faster than ever and with technologies that are more complex than ever. Teamwork – and in many cases global teams – are essential to the development of these technologies and teamwork depends for its success on effective management processes such as the TTM model. Though mature in product development, processes for managing technology innovation are a relatively new concept. However, given that technology research and product development are now more closely coupled than ever, it is essential to develop an innovation process strategy to maximize the potential of the teams, their technology and their products.

This chapter has given an overview of some of the thinking on this strategy in place at Harlow. It has also shown the importance of understanding patterns of innovation on both a long and short timescale, and how they depart from earlier models of technology innovation.

Acknowledgements are due to the following Nortel Networks staff at Harlow Laboratories: David Adlington, Philip Hargrave, David Carter, Graham Fearnhead, Ian Gould, Chris Greenhill and Peter Sutton.

7

Leading innovation teams

THE WISDOM OF TEAMS?

'The design principle of innovation,' writes Peter Drucker, 'is the team.' He might as well have said that innovation's design principle is the project, for the two things go hand in hand.

This is the age of the team. The notion of teamwork has survived too long to be considered a fad or gimmick. Teams are here to stay. Practically any manager these days will lead a work group or a department called a 'team'. You will not survive as a manager, the received wisdom tells us, without teamworking skills.

Not everybody, though, is happy with this blanket praise for 'the wisdom of teams'. Teams may perform brilliantly but they also require a lot of maintenance, and this can make them costly. Teams may fail because managers are not trained sufficiently in the dynamics of teams – or because they are spending too much effort on teambuilding at the expense of the work to be done. Above all, teams are promoted without a clear understanding of whether the work *needs* to be organized in a team.

Here is a definition of a team. Let's examine it and see how well it stands up: *A team is a group of people working together to achieve common objectives.* Objectives, of course, might be operational or innovative. At once we can see that the word 'team' actually encompasses *two* kinds of teams. What might they look like – and how might they differ? The answer

grows out of the history of the word 'team' itself – a history full of interesting twists and turns.

TWO KINDS OF TEAMS

The word 'team' is very old. Its original meaning is 'childbearing'; from
the start the word has associations of creativity and fertility. We've entirely
lost this meaning in modern English, although we can still hear a faint
echo of it when we use the words 'teem' or 'teeming', meaning to be full
of life.

Later a 'team' came to mean a brood of animals, particularly geese or
pigs. Thence it came to describe a group of animals working together; a
team of horses ploughing, for example. This is where the idea of work
first appears in connection with the word. By the 17th century, this meaning had become applied to people as well as animals. A team of work-
men were 'harnessed' together to pull in one direction, under the
direction of a leader or foreman.

At about the same time, the word became applied to a group of people playing as one side in a game. But this new meaning is subtly different from the first. A football team, for example, is a group of people
working towards a common objective; but it is not in 'harness'. Each
player has a great deal of individual freedom of movement, which the
team as a whole must co-ordinate in complex ways to achieve their goal
(interesting that we use this word at work as well as in football!). A football team differs in other ways from the harnessed team. Each player is
a specialist; without a range of skills, the team would be impoverished
and unsuccessful. The team follows a broad strategy rather than a rigidly
imposed process. Interestingly, it is also engaged in a performance task
with a defined time limit.

So we now have two complementary definitions of teams: functional
teams and innovation teams.

In a **functional team**, a group of people performs as a 'cell' within a
larger operation. Everybody in the team is doing essentially the same kind
of work. They are equals under the guidance of a team leader. Probably

most teams at work are of this kind: a team in a call centre, an administrative team, a cell on an assembly line. Functional teams might be called departments. A finance department, a sales department, a housing department: all are functional teams.

In an **innovation team**, a group of people with diverse skills deliberately comes together to create a single result. Their work is not part of a larger operation; it is the whole task. A hospital team, for example, is drawn together to apply diverse skills to create a cured patient; a theatre company is a creative team drawn together to create a single production; an innovation project team is a multi-functional team assembled to create a new product.

1 FUNCTIONAL TEAMS – EXAMPLES

Advice teams
- Committees
- Review panels
- Quality circles
- Employee involvement groups
- Advisory councils

Production teams
- Assembly teams
- Manufacturing crews
- Mining teams
- Flight attendant crews
- Data processing groups
- Maintenance teams

2 INNOVATION TEAMS – EXAMPLES

Project teams
- Research groups
- Expeditions
- Planning teams
- Architect teams
- Product teams
- Taskforces

Action teams
- Sports teams
- Hospital teams
- Theatre groups
- Orchestras
- Negotiating teams

Some would say that functional teams aren't strictly teams at all, but work groups. They might argue that the qualities of true teamwork only come into play when the work moves out of the functional cycle and into the innovation cycle. It might be truer to say that the *balance* between functional and innovation work shifts between the four groups identified in the table above. Production teams are almost entirely functional; advice teams are highly functional but would benefit from some innovative input. Action teams are highly innovative but include a degree of functional work. Project teams are wholly innovative in orientation: they exist only for the duration of the project; once the task is achieved the team breaks up.

CASE STUDY

GUERRILLA WARFARE IN THE FIGHT AGAINST DISEASE – PATIENT CARE AT THE MAYO CLINIC, MINNESOTA

Each afternoon, in a tiny workroom on the 12th floor of the Mayo Clinic, the battle against cancer begins with a conversation. At 1pm, staff at the world-famous clinic in Rochester, Minnesota, line the walls of the room with x-rays and 'CAT' scans from the current caseload. The space fills with a small crowd of cancer specialists, surgeons, residents and nurses. For the next three hours, this talented team will debate the condition and treatment of the day's patients.

This scene typifies patient care at the Mayo Clinic. At many hospitals, a patient may spend weeks going from one specialist to another, receiving separate diagnoses and maddeningly divergent advice – only to wait even longer for surgery. At Mayo, specialists don't just visit the patient, they 'swarm' them; diagnosing a complex problem, proposing treatment and often booking the patient for surgery within 24 hours of the diagnosis.

In an industry that is dominated by increasingly powerful technology, teamwork is Mayo's biggest innovation. To be sure, other medical institutions use teams. But Mayo has incorporated collaborative methods into everything that it does – from diagnosis and surgery to policy making, strategic planning and leadership. At Mayo, the art of medicine is the epitome of teamwork.

CREATING THE PROJECT TEAM

The best innovation project teams are energized by creativity and curiosity. They understand that current reality will change and that change is their ally, not their enemy. They are willing to evolve and co-evolve with their working environment. The challenge for the project manager is to mould this team, quickly.

QUALITIES OF A SUCCESSFUL PROJECT TEAM

✓ Commitment to the project.
✓ Result-oriented attitude.
✓ Creative thinking.
✓ Willingness to change.
✓ Concern for quality.
✓ Ability to predict trends.
✓ High involvement, interest and energy.
✓ Capacity to resolve conflict quickly.
✓ Good communications and feedback.
✓ Mutual trust and confidence.
✓ Interest in self-development.
✓ Effective organizational interfacing.

What, then, are you seeking to create in a project team? What does an effective innovation project team look like? Think about a project team in terms of three key areas.

- Task
- Identity
- Skills.

First, an effective project understands its **task**. It should have full responsibility for the complete task. The task should be time-limited: there should be a firm deadline, at which point the project must be seen to have delivered what it promised. And the team must understand that responsibility for achieving the task is collective.

Secondly, the team should develop a distinct **identity**. That identity is defined primarily by the task: it's not a matter simply of printing t-shirts or sending the team on outward-bound teambuilding courses. The team's identity gives it its reason for existing and places it in the context of the host organization. It should be outward-looking. Focusing on the final outcome of the project will help to maintain team commitment without isolating it dangerously from the wider strategy of the organization. The

---

MOTIVATING YOUR PROJECT TEAM

✓ Involve all the team in the planning process.
✓ Ensure they all understand their action responsibilities in the project.
✓ Learn about team members' skills, experience, expectations and needs.
✓ Involve them in problem solving and seek their ideas and suggestions.
✓ Keep everyone well informed of progress, including all stakeholders.
✓ Help team members to schedule and prioritize their workload when necessary.
✓ Establish a decision-taking process and seek consensus from the team.
✓ Review performance regularly through 1:1 meetings and set targets.
✓ Establish a motivating climate and hold regular, short team meetings.
✓ Resolve conflicts and grievances promptly.
✓ Celebrate success and learn from the failures.

project manager has a particular responsibility to reinforce the team's identity by leadership: reminding the team continually of the project goals and the importance of achieving them.

Finally, a successful project team is characterized by a diverse set of **skills**. The project team's diversity should be its strength. That strength is developed through the interplay of people's skills in pursuit of the project's goal. The project manager must develop, in particular, the team's ability to think together. It is not enough to assemble a group of disparate specialists with clearly identified action responsibilities. A project – and an innovation project above all – demands more. The team must be able to think creatively, constructively and coherently. It must be ready to exchange ideas and share information, work together towards decisions and adapt to changes in circumstances. It must be able to hold productive conversations.

The project's success will depend critically on the project manager's ability to weld this diverse group into a coherent team. They must energize and direct the team to give high performance, willingly, throughout the project life.

MANAGING THE PROJECT

The project window appears as soon as you are appointed project manager. It may at first appear quite small.

- The project data available are limited, often just a general description or 'Terms of Reference', which may be supported by a feasibility study carried out much earlier.
- The project specification may be vague. Minimal planning may have been carried out; in an innovation project, nobody may know exactly what is involved in achieving success.
- The project will certainly have some objectives, although these are not always immediately obvious. The stated objectives are often unclear and sometimes even misguided.
- Availability of resources has probably received little attention but somebody may have set a budget limit.

So your view through the window is very limited. The information available is constrained by the views of those who first thought up the project. You will have many distractions at this point, principally day-to-day operational activities. These have to continue and your project role is an additional burden, which can lead to extra stress.

If the project is to start well, you have to move closer to the window. The view may be confusing and hazy. You must consider the resources available and define the project's objective as clearly as possible. The next major leap forward is the key to the success of the whole project. It is made up of two giant steps:

- putting the project in context; and
- identifying all those with an interest in the project.

PUTTING THE PROJECT IN CONTEXT

Both you and the project team need to be clear on the context of the project in the organization.

- How does the project fit into corporate strategy?
- Why is it necessary?
- What has been done before?
- What is the real purpose of the project?
- Why are you selected for the project?
- What will you gain from the project if it succeeds?
- What happens if you fail?
- What will the organization gain from the project?
- What are the expectations of the senior management?

Getting answers to these and other questions creates a vision for the project and removes some of the haze in the project window. The answers will help to motivate the team and clarify their contributions. They will begin to understand the reasons behind the project and the risks involved in tackling it.

IDENTIFYING THOSE WITH AN INTEREST IN THE PROJECT

Anyone who has an interest in the project's outcome is a stakeholder. This starts with you and the team: your interest is obvious. But there will always be others with a vested interest in all or parts of the project life cycle as well as its results. You can't ignore them; in many cases, you will want to cultivate them.

Every innovation project should have a sponsor, a senior manager who is directly sponsoring the project and is accountable at senior level. Identify this sponsor and get to know them quickly. With the help of your team, you must then assess all the other possible stakeholders. All of them will have different perceptions of the project's purpose and expectations of its outcome. All have a contribution to make. What is more, stakeholders will bring their own agenda, values, styles and aspirations to the project.

Stakeholders fall into two groups. You must first secure the support and commitment of the **internal** stakeholders. Politics will always influence the degree of co-operation you will be able to achieve across functional boundaries. Your project has to compete for resources with other projects, as well as with day-to-day operations. Other managers may believe they should lead your project because they could do a better job. This element of competition and resentment may create difficult relationships and conflict.

The **external** stakeholders may include the end user and client (who may not be the same), the local community, external institutions, suppliers, consultants and contractors. Their influence may be central or on the fringes, either at the start or much later in the project life cycle.

Managing all of these stakeholders may be the most difficult challenge you will face in running a project. You have limited authority over most of them and you may find it difficult to influence them to your advantage. Nonetheless, you must find a way to manage these stakeholders effectively so that they remain positive in supporting both you and your project.

DON'T BE SO THEATRICAL?

Theatre can teach other industries a great deal about how to manage the innovation process and innovation teams. A theatrical production provides an interesting blueprint for any innovation team. Theatre companies also vividly illustrate the dynamic relationship between operational and innovation work.

The structure of a theatre company reflects the division between operational and innovation work with startling clarity. Most companies will have a small administrative base – management, box office, marketing – whose responsibility is the ongoing maintenance of the company. If the company is based in a building, it may also have a small number of technical departments – lighting, make-up, scenery construction, props – that work only in relation to specific productions. But the core of the company's work is a sequence of creative projects. A project team will be assembled for each, made up of technicians, actors, musicians and designers, led by a director. The director may be the artistic director of the company, doubling up as project leader and functional manager, or an outsider contracted solely to create the production.

Theatre productions share a number of characteristics with other innovation projects.

- **They are time-limited.** Every production is a self-contained project with an immovable deadline – the opening night.
- **They are resource-specific.** Each production is budgeted separately. Very few resources will be permanent: perhaps a building and certain technical equipment. Most of the team engaged in the production will be on fixed-term contracts.
- **They are multidisciplinary.** The success of any production depends on the diverse skills of the whole team.

The director of the production must manage this team skilfully and creatively. They must also manage the web of external stakeholders in the project: the theatre's board of directors, sponsors, administrative staff, the local authority and funding bodies. The most important stakeholders, of course, are the audience: they may include educational groups, the Friends of the theatre, corporate parties and the press.

The progress of a production is also an object lesson in structuring an innovation project. This aspect of theatrical practice usually happens behind closed doors and is relatively unknown.

- The production will start with a specific **goal**. In management terms, this is the production's 'mission'. Usually, the mission is represented by a script written by a playwright. The script is a starting point: a set of instructions to the team to set them going. Some productions may start in another way: the desire to dramatize a book, for example, or a set of improvizations based on some local issue or historical event. The production will almost certainly have a name that identifies it; the aim of the project is to realize what the name represents in some creative and entertaining way.
- Next, a **team** is gathered together. The size and composition of the team will depend, of course, on the perceived needs of the project. Actors will be cast, a director appointed, a designer chosen – perhaps a composer contracted.
- The project is opened with a meeting that delivers the **vision** of the project. The entire team assembles, perhaps for a single day, to meet and celebrate the start of the project. This is something of a ritual, a moment of great significance when the team first finds out about each other and starts out on the journey towards the opening night. The vision of the project is made concrete for all to see. An important element of this event is the viewing of the production designs; the designer shows a model of the set and costume designs and usually gives a short presentation.
- Next, a period of **rehearsal**. With the vision of the production in mind, and an eye on the ever-looming deadline, everybody on the team works hard to deliver their contribution. The great danger at this stage is that different parts of the team will work in isolation; frequent meetings may be necessary to maintain the shared vision of the production

and to ensure that acting, music, design and lighting are developing consistently.

- The next ritualistic event is the **technical rehearsal**. All aspects of the production are assembled for the first time. Slowly, often painfully slowly, they are fitted together.
- With luck, the production may have a number of **previews**. These are performances that are also rehearsals. An audience is invited to watch the show, often for free or at a reduced rate, on the understanding that the work is not yet complete.
- Finally, the production opens on **opening night**. The project is essentially complete; although it may grow and change during subsequent performances, the production must be in a fit state to present to the paying public for this performance. This is also a highly ritualized event; team members send each other cards and flowers and often celebrate with a party after the performance.

This is a project schedule in all but name. Every one of these stages in the production process finds a corollary in the life of an innovation proj-

THEATRICAL PRACTICE AS INNOVATION – A COMPARISON CHECKLIST

Theatrical production	Innovation project
✓ Mission	✓ Complete task
✓ Gathering the team – casting, etc	✓ Gather a diverse team
✓ Vision (design)	✓ Provide a vision
✓ Rehearsal	✓ Practise skills
✓ Technical rehearsal	✓ Put it all together before 'going live'
✓ Previews	✓ Pilot or test
✓ Performance	✓ Deadline
✓ Monitor audience reaction	✓ Monitor customer reaction

ect. Every innovation project should be organized as a complete task, from inception to rollout. It will demand the diverse skills of a multi-functional team, who will need to find ways of working productively together. The project will only have a chance of succeeding if it has a powerful vision of what it is aiming for; the more powerful the vision, the more committed will be the project team. There must be a clear protocol for managing the progress of the project. And the deadline, the point by which a result is expected, should have the quality of an opening night; the team needs to feel a real urgency about completing on time.

CASE STUDY

CREATING COLLECTIVELY – TEAMWORK IN THÉÂTRE DE COMPLICITÉ

Théâtre de Complicité has elevated teamwork to a high degree of sophistication. The results are innovative theatre pieces that have been internationally acclaimed. Complicité was founded in 1983 by Simon McBurney, Annabel Arden and Marcello Magni. So far, the company has 27 productions to its credit, performed in more than 180 towns in 41 countries on four continents.

The company breaks the mould in terms of the way it creates theatre. Traditionally, a production is dominated by two individuals: the playwright and the director. The playwright creates a script; the director interprets it. Everybody else – actors, musicians, technicians, designers – works within the guidelines set by these two figures. Theatre directors have become increasingly powerful; the director of a production is a project manager in all but name.

Complicité challenges all that. For a start, they challenge the need to start with a script. Although they have mounted productions of traditionally written scripts – *The Chairs* by Ionesco, Brecht's *Caucasian Chalk Circle* – most of their work starts life as short stories or other kinds of text. Combining elements is a defining feature of Complicité's style: overlapping texts to create new resonances, collaborating with artists in different media (a recent production about Shostakovich involved the Emerson string quartet). Music, physical action, visual imagery and text come together to create a theatre that is disturbing and vital.

Teamwork is central to this method of creation. Every piece of work is a collective enterprise. Typical is a recent production, *The Man in the Ice*. The work began with a number of stories and literary influences: principally, Konrad Spindler's book of the same name. 'We took the inspiration for a lot of our work from that,' explains McBurney. 'The book suggests a number of explanations for the perfect preservation of a human body for 5,200 years in the Alps: human, geological and scientific. Looking closely at the case, we began to explore more deeply our thoughts about this subject and, in the end, about ourselves. Spindler looks at objects, and at the body itself, to find out about this man's life. Very quickly, as we rehearsed, it become clear that it was our common humanity that connected us to the Ice Man; that this link was physical and written in our collective memory. The Ice Man is himself a memory aid; this very old body led us back, far in time, forcing us to reconsider the past, to redefine what matters in our lives.'

Out of the specific details of this story, a vision emerges. 'Very soon it became clear that this piece was going to be about journeys: across Europe, across time, across memory and across our sense of ourselves. The idea of travelling, of setting out on a voyage, is basic – primordial. On the one hand, you have this final journey that the Ice Man takes across the mountains; on the other, you could think of the stories of immigration in the last century. The vast number of these stories that emerged during the first few weeks of rehearsal reinforced the idea that the work was becoming polyphonic – multi-voiced, multi-layered. A lot of rehearsal was about finding the style that would allow us to express these stories in some way simultaneously.'

After seven weeks of rehearsal (out of a total of ten), the company had found five main narratives and 18 secondary stories. Then came the need to carve out a clear structure. 'Adopting a very fluid playing style, you risk confusion,' explains McBurney. 'Inevitably, our work led us towards consolidating the material. Certain things emerge as essential, others less so. It is hard to describe this process; in the end, it's instinctive.'

McBurney's comments on the process reflect the complexities of any innovation project. 'It's this informal side of the process I find fascinating,' says McBurney. 'Nobody really ever had any overall idea of the plan of the piece. When I started out on the work, I saw myself as a kind of rehearsal co-ordinator. I had about 20 ideas for structure. I worked in parallel with the actors; when they looked at the scientific aspects of the material, I did the same. A lot of what I created we didn't use, but some elements came to play a part in a later stage of the work.'

Creativity comes through teamwork. Day by day, the actors teased out their ideas, each one preparing pieces to present to the others. This interweaving of ideas became part of the refining process, capturing the essential element in each situation.

Launching the work was not a one-off event. Over time, more and more bits of the work were performed. 'First of all with a very limited audience, made up essentially of friends and collaborators. These people themselves took part in the work, playing a key role in establishing its final form. These little performances were stimulating; the actors had to bring to them all the intensity of a real performance. It's an excellent discipline.'

McBurney insists on the importance of the actors' input. 'They bring everything to the piece. To begin with, it's a matter of establishing the context that allows them to go on their journey. An atmosphere of encouragement and freedom is essential. Collaboration demands time, trust, patience, openness, accessibility, concentration and creativity. Through deep reading, observation and improvization, the creative team has fused their experience, their histories, with the Ice Man's story. The actors had to think about every aspect of the project; they had to find interesting ideas to bring the rehearsals to life. They might have had to ponder theories of time, philosophy and maths. They even had to study different scientific textbooks. We've thought through ideas about archaeology, thought and memory. We've been led towards chaos theory, towards complexity. This process demands lots of patience and attention. Such deep study might seem extravagant, but it led to a rich body of knowledge that enlivened the process.'

This unusual approach certainly seems to work. Complicité has won more than 25 international prizes for its work. The writer John Berger sums up their achievement. 'Theatre de Complicité,' he writes, 'ignores frontiers and crosses them without passports.'

Theatrical practice – particularly the kind of innovative practice embodied by companies such as Complicité – suggests a number of questions for innovation project managers.

- **Does the project have a clear identity?** What is the project's 'vision'? Do you have a clear enough idea of what you are setting out to achieve? That identity should be strong enough to withstand the inevitable complexities and ambiguities that will arise as the project proceeds.
- **Is your team up to the job?** Have you gathered the right people for the job? Are their roles and responsibilities clear? Are they aware of their relationships to each other; their own tasks and how these fit with the tasks of other team members? Are they willing to take on the learning, the risks, the collaboration, the patience, that the project will

demand? How do you propose to build the team around the project and gain the team's commitment to unforeseen work?

- **How will you communicate the vision to the team?** An event would undoubtedly be useful, equivalent to the opening day of rehearsals, as the initial stage of teambuilding and to set the project firmly on its feet. Can you provide any concrete vision of the project's goal – an equivalent to the designer's model of the set or the costume drawings? Don't ignore the 'ritual' aspect of such a meeting. This initial meeting gives you the chance to instil a sense of the project's significance in your team members, and also a sense of their value as a team.
- **Have you got rich input?** McBurney's project depended on a large amount of stimulating input: ideas and information that spark ideas in the team and send the team into new and unexplored territory. Don't expect the team to have ideas in a vacuum. Where *else* are you looking for ideas?
- **What is your role as project manager?** What kind of leadership do you intend to practise? McBurney sees his role as a co-ordinator, fine-tuning input in pursuit of a vision. If you have too clear a sense of what you are trying to innovate, the team will not be able to contribute to its growth.
- **How will you plan the project?** Planning in too much detail may stifle the creativity that emerges from collaborative work. The point of the project is to create something; to develop an increasingly clear embodiment of your initial vision. Plans cannot and should not be worked out in fine detail at the very start. All plans are provisional; the whole point of planning the project is to have a plan you can alter. Project members must be able to communicate with the kind of intensity and patience that McBurney's actors displayed to keep the project alive. Pay particular attention to the fact that different members of the team may be working independently on different aspects of the project. You will need to build into your schedule regular meetings and other opportunities to check progress.
- **How will you put it all together?** Do you have plans for launching

or completing the project? Have you built in enough testing time? Don't try to make sense of everything too soon. McBurney's team worked for seven weeks out of ten before trying to put the whole production together. Be patient. Give first-stage thinking enough time.

- **Can you 'preview' the innovation?** You could run a pilot, or launch the product in selected local areas before launching globally. You may well benefit from involving your customers in the pre-launch phase.
- **When's the opening night?** This can be the hardest element to transfer from the theatrical setting into the context of an innovation project. An absolute deadline concentrates minds wonderfully; necessity is indeed often the mother of invention. In the theatre, opening night is opening night; it has been advertised and tickets have been sold. To postpone is to announce failure. Most innovation projects, in contrast, can usually be extended. If the team knows this, energy can dissipate and creativity evaporate. Can you impose some form of external deadline that matters to the team: a public announcement of the launch, perhaps, or an appearance at an important trade show? Also, don't forget the value of a 'first-night party'; a celebration of the project's achievement that acknowledges the team's hard work and emotional commitment.

A successful project team rarely forms spontaneously. It must be worked for. View the team as a community, rather than as a functional unit. De-emphasize the operational rules that people normally work by; encourage people to find alternatives for 'the way we always do things around here'. The diversity of your team is its greatest strength: encourage differences of opinion and invest in multiple interpretations of reality. Practise dialogue and explore how to make team conversations less adversarial and more creative. Make information accessible to the team.

The project itself is the strongest element in building the team. In theatrical jargon, 'the play's the thing'. The project comes first. This sometimes means making unpopular decisions in the interest of the project.

Keep the team focused on the project, and on its deadline. Respect team members' input and praise them for it. Give them the opportunity to present their work *during* the project, not just at its completion. Lead from behind; let them see that the project's success is *their* responsibility, not merely yours.

The sorcerer's apprentice – training interventions to inspire innovation

GILLIAN BARKER

Gillian Barker is Managing Partner of Direction, a learning consultancy. She is particularly interested in creativity and arts-based training. Gillian has extensive experience in education and the arts, and has recently developed Creativity at Work, a new public course for a leading training organization. She has degrees in English, education and art history, and is continuing post-graduate work in art history.

Strange tales sometimes emerge from organizations, and from the conference centres where managers gather. Some seem too odd to take seriously. Chief executives playing in sandpits? Musicians, storytellers, actors and artists infiltrating the business world to galvanize the creativity of middle management?

It seems that these stories are often true. The relationship between the creative arts and business, once characterized by mutual suspicion, is changing. A company's cultural kudos was once enhanced by its arts sponsorship: investing in a corporate art collection, for example. Now, you have to be *doing* it. Teambuilding events are as likely these days to involve making pictures or writing a play as white-water rafting or assault courses. A great deal of training goes into 'releasing the creative potential of people at work'. The question is: How effective is it?

CASE STUDY

DOODLING YOUR WAY TO SUCCESS – ARTS-BASED TRAINING IN NORTH CAROLINA

Managers are often asked to do strange things to inspire their teams. But taking up drawing is not usually one of them.

Yet at the Center for Creative Leadership in Greensboro, North Carolina, that's exactly what they are doing. David Horth and Charles Palus, who work at the centre, explain that modern business demands leadership that is 'creative and contagious, capable of inspiring and sustaining creativity throughout an organization.' They add that innovation management is all too often a bolt-on or afterthought, or confined to managers in R&D.

Managers at the centre draw, create collages, and write poetry, stories and music. They even interpret each other's dreams. The result, claim Horth and Palus, is that they can explore their own problems in a more rounded way.

For example, they worked with a team seeking to deal with a long-standing product problem. The centre's approach showed them that the problem, far from being merely technical, was ingrained in the organization's culture. Fear and anxiety about change were impeding progress towards a solution. Seeing the complexities of the situation helped the team come up with a more comprehensive approach.

It's all about balancing the two sides of our thinking. Most management sees itself as rational and analytical. Finding the hidden intuitive and imaginative skills allows managers to take a more 'whole-brain' approach. And it might all start with a doodle.

CREATIVITY – THE SLUMBERING GIANT

People in organizations are increasingly aware that they have left their creativity, along with the rest of their cultural baggage, at the workplace door. Participants on creativity courses often say that they feel that they are working in a vacuum. Although creativity is often said to be desirable in their organization, their organizations lack the means for it to flourish.

An historical shadow looms over this paradoxical situation. Industrialization separated functional and creative work. The assembly line epitomizes the problem of injecting creativity into strictly organized processes. But it is replicated in many other kinds of work: the bureaucracy of a complex administrative process in banking or the government; distribution networks and 'just-in-time' systems within assembly and retail businesses. Indeed, the very structures of our organizations bear witness to the division between creative work at the higher, strategic levels, and uncreative, functional work at the lower levels.

As a result, organizational creativity has been sidelined. It has become viewed as a singular, somewhat odd process – a great idea but difficult to fit into the scheme of things.

Tudor Rickards, in his book *Creativity and the Management of Change*, has called creativity 'the slumbering giant of organizational studies'.

The notion of creativity at the individual level, in contrast, is alive and well. Bookshelves marked 'Popular Psychology' or 'Mind, Body and Spirit' groan with books about harnessing inner resources in order to think, work and live more effectively. These vary greatly in quality; some have their uses. Their popularity indicates that many of us feel we could all be drawing on parts of our imagination we might normally ignore. It's tempting to reach for the nearest technique. This may be a successful tactic for individuals, but an organizational approach to developing creativity needs to be more thorough and broad-based.

What can training do to help? How can a training intervention inspire individuals and teams to think and act more creatively? Can training help an organization to develop creativity as part of its culture? What should we be trying to train, anyway? And what exactly is this thing we so glibly call 'creativity'?

CREATIVE THINKING AND CREATIVE ACTION

Creativity straddles the divide between the abstract and the practical. This divide is one of the main features of our educational system. On one side of the chasm sits abstract, analytical thought; on the other, practical action. The first is associated with power, intellectual achievement and status, the second with vocational training and more or less manual labour. Yet I have found, again and again, that the best abstract ideas come from very practical people. People are able to bridge the gap between ideas and action; but life in organizations – and particularly the life of the manager – gives few opportunities to make the leap.

Management, a relatively recent development in the way we organize work, is a practical art. Yet it's increasingly portrayed as an intellectual discipline. Managers who think about and study for MBAs find themselves struggling in this mental divide between the virtues of decisive action and the seductive allure of the latest theory.

Creativity, in this context, becomes 'creative thinking'. But the demon of the quick fix – the simple, 'practical' solution that produces instant results – demands that such thinking is fast and essentially easy. 'Difficulty' is the really dirty word. As a result, in creativity as in so much business training, there is a tendency towards the faddish and superficial. Trainers – working within the constraints of the short course – peddle various tricks and exercises designed to help trainees 'think outside the box'. Such techniques are, in my view, pretty harmless; but they rarely have any long-lasting effect. And the benefits felt by individuals may not translate into benefits for those working around them (see boxed example opposite).

There is no quick fix. It is not just a question of people learning a creative technique in a day; it is a question of addressing the place of creativity within the whole culture of an organization. Unless people are encouraged to work on specific creative tasks – practically – then the so-

ON YOUR CARPET – WHEN A TRAINING IDEA GOES WRONG

I was told recently of a person attending a course on managing stress. Various creative approaches were suggested to her. One was the 'Flying Carpet': 'When everything gets too much,' she was told, 'imagine you are flying away on your magic carpet.'

This image appealed to her so much that she employed it frequently, to the extent that she showed a marked reluctance to return to work (on her carpet, of course).

Her colleagues, much to their own irritation, were left dealing with all the off-loaded stress.

called creativity conjured up on creative thinking courses will be purposeless. So I have no objection to chief executives playing in sandpits, but I would ask them two questions. What good ideas are generated from this practical activity? How are these ideas informing the creative approach to a specific task you have in front of you?

Trainers often find themselves resorting to the inappropriate, the superficial and the cosmetic – through no fault of their own. They have little time to lay out their stall of creative techniques in the jostling marketplace. Over a day or two, it is possible to give people a taste of how effective certain approaches can be. But it is only a taste, a brief experience at most. It may lead people to access their creativity in the longer term, and hopefully in the workplace. But this is merely dressing Cinderella for the ball; to get there, she needs transport, and that is innovation. Innovation is the implementation of creativity. The task of the creativity trainer, it seems to me, is to prepare people for innovation.

BRAINSTORMING – HELP OR HINDRANCE?

Brainstorming is one of the best known techniques to stimulate ideas. It has all the features that make it attractive to trainers: it is a structured technique with clear rules that can be applied quickly. It has, however, had a mixed press throughout its history, and people in organizations are often ambivalent about its effectiveness. Like any other technique, it all depends on how you do it. Brainstorming has come to be regarded by many as a free-for-all, chuck-anything-in-the-pot-and-see-what-comes-out session. On a good day, it may be productive; but, as anyone who has tried it knows, it quite often isn't.

When brainstorming isn't working, it is usually for an obvious reason. Often, people simply don't understand what they are supposed to be doing. The basic rules are quite specific:

- suspend judgement;
- be as unconventional as you can;
- combine and improve on ideas; and
- more is better.

Following these simple rules should in itself help to make the session more productive.

Above all, the trainer needs to make it abundantly and continually clear that creative thinking is *not* operational thinking. The rules and standards that apply to one can be damaging in the other. Merely pointing out that operational thinking is inappropriate while generating ideas often dramatically liberates people who have been slogging through sessions where ideas are strangled at birth by variations of 'it won't work'. The fun of generating wild and wacky ideas seems to become more meaningful when participants understand that these ideas open the door to the potential of ideas generally, that they are useful because they can shift perception, not that we are going to implement mad and impractical suggestions.

Brainstorming can also be afflicted with what trainers call 'interpersonal' problems. Our readiness to offer ideas can be stifled by concerns

MAKING BRAINSTORMING MORE EFFECTIVE

Experience suggests that a few other simple disciplines can make a big difference to the session's effectiveness.

- The discipline of 'scoring' can produce more ideas and help crazier ideas to surface. A target of between 50 and 100 ideas in ten minutes is not unreasonable for a competent team of about seven people.
- The structure of the session might be varied by:
  - briefing the team with the problem a day beforehand, to allow for private musing and 'sleeping on the problem';
  - beginning the session with a warm-up exercise, unrelated to the task in hand; and
  - taking breaks between techniques, to allow people's minds to relax and discover new ideas.
- Alternate individual and group thinking. An idea is only ever the product of a single mind. Solitary thinking is best for having ideas; group thinking for building on them. Brainstorming can benefit from using both. Ask people to generate ideas individually to begin the process. Gather them anonymously, to encourage the wilder ideas to surface and counter any politics or inhibitions in the team. Then use group brainstorming to group the ideas, build on them, combine them, vary them, develop them and transform them.

about status, identity, and by personal and political inhibitions. These concerns must be addressed first for ideas to begin percolating. Creating the right atmosphere is vital, though not always easy. The brainstorming session undermined by politics is a classic example of how creative work needs a foundation of good operational functioning. If it is superimposed on a dysfunctional group, then it will only serve to highlight the dysfunction all the more.

CREATIVITY AS WORK

Creativity can be subversive and hard to control. Our understanding of how to harness it within organizations is still pretty crude. Very few organizations have any policy regarding creativity, still fewer have any internal structure allowing creativity to be integrated. If you begin to train creativity in an organization, you invariably at some level come to this sticking point. And it is at this point where a conscious decision must be made by the person or people in whom organizational power resides not only to allow room for creativity, but to put structures in place to make for its continued integration.

So what's to do? Creativity might well reveal itself as the capricious element in our thought processes; but it is work, nevertheless. Managers are only likely to make space for creativity if they can see it as a process to be managed like any other. Perhaps those of us who train creativity need to turn our attention away from creative thinking towards the process of creating itself.

CREATIVITY AS PLAY

We have very little understanding of how creativity actually works. It seems that we can understand 'talent' to some extent, and we can recognize creative products – inventions, works of art, new theories. But what happens in between is still a mystery. Neither depth nor behavioural psychology has had much of groundbreaking interest to say about creativity. Depth psychology tends towards a reductionist view of creativity, often regarding it as a compensatory activity. Behavioural psychology has tended to look at the peripherals of creativity: to a consideration of what are seen to be the 'traits' of a creative person. The only writer I have found who tackles the creative moment, and seeks to analyze it as a process, is Rollo May.

May describes the creative process as 'bringing something new into birth'. In a paper published as long ago as 1958, he distinguishes between what he calls 'pseudo-creativity' – an exhibitionist, escapist form of creativity – and 'genuine' creativity, where there is an 'encounter' with reality. In the one, a person may enjoy their creative 'talent' but not actually create anything; in the other, a real creative product appears in the world. May suggests that 'it is not strictly proper to speak of "a creative person" but only of *a creative act*, the person creating.' The essence of creativity is in the 'intensity of the encounter'; the power and depth with which we engage with reality. Creativity is not truly itself unless it becomes active, encountering external reality and having a reciprocal relationship with it. This is true, May suggests, not just of artistic creativity, but also of scientific and philosophical creativity – and indeed of any kind of work that 'brings something new into birth'.

Play, for Rollo May, is the prototype of this encounter. It has all the features of the act of creating. Trainers can reflect on how they might integrate some of them into their own work, and how the characteristics of play might be transferred to the process of innovation itself.

- **Play is voluntary.** We can't play to order. We don't *have* to play; we can stop at any time. Play is driven by curiosity, but is also disinterested; it exists beyond the satisfaction of immediate needs or purposeful work. It is an interlude in life. Yet play is also an integral part of life; it satisfies a deep natural need in all of us, for meaning and for belonging. Perhaps that is why children respond particularly keenly to playing in natural environments.

- **Play is not real life.** We step out of ordinary life to play. But 'only pretending' doesn't mean that play is frivolous. Far from it. Play casts a spell; it is characterized by *absorption*. It has definite objectives. When children play, particularly on their own but also with others, they often become completely absorbed in what they are doing. If you can remember that state of absorption when you were a child, making dens perhaps, then you have in mind a microcosm of a creative act. Adults, of course, can also become absorbed in a task; but functional work tends to be characterized more by disruption and interruptions than by quiet, focused concentration. Training gives us a powerful opportunity to recreate that quiet, absorbed state, if only briefly.

- **Play is secluded.** Play exists in its own time and place. It begins, and then at a certain moment it ends. It also happens in a special area: a playground or pitch, a stage or a magic circle, a private spot where intrusions from the real world are unwelcome. It is important to recreate that sense of a special time and place in any training event that hopes to stimulate creativity.

- **Play creates order.** Play brings a sense of harmony and perfection to the chaos of the real world. But it is not static. Play is intensely alive and active. It develops a wide range of types of intelligence, through problem solving, improvization, metaphor and cultural input from outside. Discovery comes from doing. Play uses whatever is to hand, combining different elements into new forms. The beauty of play is often expressed through tension and release. All games have this quality: whether seeking to get a game of patience 'out' or winning a football match. Drama and music, storytelling and even visual art all encompass this dynamic or tension and resolution. This is a tension that trainers can exploit.

- **Play has its own rules.** External measurements of performance, profit and effectiveness are low considerations. Play's main purpose is to create pleasure. But break the rules and you might be called a cheat or, worse, a spoilsport. Cheating may be acceptable; the spoilsport, on the other hand, is usually given short shrift. Trainers need to establish clear rules for any creative play that they ask people to engage in.

- **Play creates community.** Games tend to generate clubs or cliques. Children tend to form teams and gangs; grown-ups form clans of like-minded people who share an appreciation of the rules and a vision of what the play signifies. Creativity training always runs the risk of creating an isolated 'clan' within an organization, and can come to be seen as 'basket weaving' – a potentially divisive activity separate from the rest of the organization.

- **Play tends to surround itself with an air of privacy, even secrecy.** Play is different. The ordinary rules of life are suspended. We might dress up to play or lock ourselves away. Participants in a creativity session need to feel comfortable with the idea that this is private and not to be judged by the rules of the outside world.

Play is not as trivial and merely recreational as it first appears. Some of its characteristics are the very ones lacking within our organizations. Annette Karmiloff-Smith, a psychologist, describes how, when children reach a level of competence in the midst of play, they will deliberately lessen that competence in order to gain a deeper understanding of the situation. This conscious 'de-skilling' as a means to an end is in striking contrast to the prevailing ethos of 'continuous improvement' and 'bolt-on solutions' fostered in many organizations. Creativity demands 'play-ful' activity that may go strongly against the grain of performance-dominated cultures.

A further contrast between play and organizational work is in their respective attitudes to time. In the workplace, we are made conscious of time continually. It is strictly regulated: dominated by deadlines, shifts and efficiency. 'Time,' we are told, 'is the one resource that is non-renewable.' Play, in contrast, uses time as an element of the process. During play, time can seem to pass quickly or move slowly because we become unconscious of it. Children famously hate to be interrupted in their play by 'five-minute warnings' or calls to stop. It is as if another kind of consciousness comes to the fore, unconstrained by the need for results, more ruminative and reflective.

Play teaches us that this kind of consciousness is vital for creative work. Trying to gallop through the full gamut of creative techniques is of limited use. Reflective consciousness allows us to access a different kind of perception, in which the mind feels allowed to make connections. Once again, play teaches a lesson that many in organizations may find hard to take: that creativity requires us to slow down, look around and wait for the mind to do its work.

Visualization techniques can encourage play as a means to release creativity. By removing thinking from the verbal arena – and by eliminating any concern for artistic skill – the trainer can encourage participants to think more freely about issues and take their ideas into new areas.

INTUITION AND THE POWER OF REFLECTION

Play is an intuitive activity. Intuition works primarily by *association*: the unconscious mind makes connections between elements to create new images or ideas. A number of thinkers have recognized the power of intuition. A highly valuable contribution comes from Guy Claxton, Visiting Professor of Psychology and Education at Bristol University. In his book, *Hare Brain, Tortoise Mind*, published in 1997, Claxton explores in depth the idea of the speed of thought. He describes how we value the 'hare brain' over the 'tortoise mind'. To be clever is to be 'quick-witted'; to be 'slow' is synonymous with being stupid. We encourage rapid, conscious thought – what he calls 'd-mode' ('d' for 'deliberation') – at the expense of slower, patient and reflective thought, which is more attuned to intuition and creativity:

> '...my argument is not just that the slow ways of knowing exist, and are useful. It is that our culture has come to ignore and undervalue them, to treat them as marginal or merely recreational, and in so doing has foreclosed on areas of our psychological resources that we need.'

Claxton's discussion of this theme is amplified by research in cognitive science. In two chapters, particularly 'Knowing More Than We Think' and 'Having an Idea', he sets out to reiterate this theme in more detail. He refers to experiments, exercises and close definitions of the associative processes at play in the area of the mind between the conscious and the unconscious. His work spans education, culture and the world of work in a challenging and productive way. Claxton suggests that we slow down: the rush to decide must wait on the patient tread of intuition and imagination. Apart from anything else, Claxton's work helps to redress the disadvantage our speed-obsessed society places on slower thinkers. It's good news for tortoises.

METAPHOR AS AN AGENT OF CREATIVE CHANGE

Metaphor is the most potent kind of associative thinking. Poets, thinkers and scientists have made significant progress through metaphorical thought. Indeed, creativity self-help books and manuals eagerly repeat the stories of Archimedes in the bath, of Kekulé dreaming of snakes eating their own tails as a solution to the chemical composition of benzene, of Poincaré seeing the solution to a complex mathematical problem while stepping on to a bus, and so on.

At its simplest, a training exercise might stimulate metaphorical thinking by using an oracle. This is no more than a random list of words, one or more of which can be juxtaposed with the issue being worked on. Juxtaposing the challenge of creating a new product with the word 'marriage', for example, might intuitively suggest metaphors of marriage between a company and its customers or suppliers, or between products, or between different production processes. The metaphor of marriage might, further, provide deeper or more systematic insights into the ideas stimulated by suggesting a 'virtual world' of marriage.

How does a metaphor work? Spanish philosopher Ortega y Gasset calls it 'probably the most fertile power possessed by man'. In *Phenomenology and Art*, he explains how metaphors transform themselves in the mind. He suggests that we use metaphor best as a means of creating a new 'mental object': a new agent of creative change that can carry a powerful emotional charge for the person discovering it. Our minds seem to be already structured for metaphor. It is essentially private. Dreams, for example, operate metaphorically. Learning through metaphor is noticeably more profound when the trainee lands on a metaphor that resounds for them personally.

We tend to take metaphors too literally in training sessions. Participants often find themselves slipping into superficial and obvious comparisons, partly because the trainer is asking them to work consciously and – inevitably – at speed. One way to counter this particular tendency is to discipline the metaphorical thinking a little. We can invoke different 'worlds' of metaphor; these worlds can be broadly categorized as organic and inorganic (see below). If the process or task being considered is 'organic' or people-centred, the trainer can encourage the participant to find a metaphor from an 'inorganic' world; if technical or systems-based, an 'organic' world can be considered. Switching radically between worlds can provide more interesting and provocative metaphors.

We need discrimination, then, when working with metaphor in organizational training. Trainers and consultants should beware of importing

VIRTUAL WORLDS

These 'worlds' of metaphor can provide a discipline for more creative metaphorical ideas.

Organic	Inorganic
Biology	Physics
Tribal customs	Mineralogy
Sports	Woodworking
Fashion	Chemistry
Dancing	Mathematics
War	Electricity
History	Astronomy
Mythology	Machines
Botany	Rocks
Philosophy	Metalworking
Theatre	Oceanography
Education	Geology
Animals	Architecture
Politics	Meteorology
Racing	Bridges
Espionage	Aeronautics
Comedy	Transport
Agriculture	Acoustics
Finance	Archaeology
Science fiction	Time and space

metaphors. Although our clients may find our metaphors stimulating and exciting, they might in the end do less than good. In the cultural vacuum that so many organizations inhabit, people become vulnerable to simplistic metaphors. Consultants, for example, who offer metaphors of organizational states in terms of Greek myths may actually impoverish people's thinking by excluding the riches of their own internal metaphors.

A METAPHOR FOR WORK?

Could we create a metaphor for the creative process itself? Perhaps it would help us grasp it more clearly.

Every age describes creativity in its own terms. We are now emerging from information technology metaphors of computer-like 'connections' within the mind to metaphors drawn from the excitements of the new sciences: quantum theory, chaos and complexity theory. But we still seem to be stuck in the rut of thinking about *applying* creativity to work.

Perhaps we should instead seek metaphors that redefine the nature of work itself. For example, we might think of work as harnessing energy.

The Sorcerer's Apprentice – the story of the apprentice who unwittingly releases the energies of creation in his master's absence – is a familiar tale that plays on this very idea of harnessing a force. (Some readers might be acquainted with Disney's retelling of the tale in *Fantasia*, in which Mickey Mouse plays the apprentice.) This story has much to say to people in organizations that lack creativity. Here, there is too much creativity, rather than not enough. In an old English folklore version of this tale, *The Master and his Pupil*, the creativity is indeed a slumbering giant: one of the most fearsome and powerful.

It is important to stress that Beelzebub in this tale stands for raw undisciplined energy – nothing devilish!

THE MASTER AND THE PUPIL

There was once a learned man 'acquainted with all the mysteries of creation'. In his secret chamber, he performed alchemical experiments and kept a great book containing 'all the secrets of the spiritual world'. One day, he left on a journey, forgetting to lock the great clasp on his volume of secrets.

In his absence, his apprentice entered the master's chamber and opened the book. At once, in sulphurous smoke, the spirit of Beelzebub appeared in terrifying flames.

'Set me a task!' he roared.

The boy didn't know what to do.

'Water yon flower,' he stammered.

Off went the spirit and returned, time and time again, with barrel-loads of water, which he poured over the tiny plant. Soon, the water was ankle-deep and, in no time at all, up to the boy's neck. The pupil had no idea how to dismiss the spirit.

Meanwhile, on his journey, the master realized he had forgotten to lock the book. He returned to the chaotic scene and uttered the magic words that sent Beelzebub back to his domain.

This story will suggest different things to different people. For me, it says three things. First, we have an understandable fear of the creative. Secondly, the creative needs to be contained and structured by a task appropriate to it. Thirdly, and most importantly, we must ask what vital connection exists between creativity and knowledge.

Innovation and knowledge management

What has innovation to do with knowledge management (KM)? In Chapter 1, we discovered three key elements of thinking that are uniquely human and contribute powerfully to our ability to innovate.

- **Memory** – the ability to store and re-use knowledge in new situations.
- **Collaboration** – the ability to think together to solve problems and generate ideas.
- **Creativity** – the ability to use what we know in new combinations.

Can knowledge management help us learn, collaborate and create?

In this chapter, we shall see that it all depends on what we mean by knowledge management – and, indeed, what we mean by 'knowledge'. We shall discover that one of the most important challenges for innovators is to find ways in which people from different disciplines and different parts of an organization can share their knowledge – and create new knowledge. We shall see that finding a common language is a vital part of the project and that learning collaboratively means paying attention to the conversations we hold to facilitate that learning.

PETER DRUCKER AND THE IDEA OF KNOWLEDGE WORK

Knowledge management is one of the fastest growing concepts in organizational theory. From being virtually unknown as a term in the early

1990s, it has become one of the most powerful buzzwords of the moment. It has even become a discrete function: many organizations now employ knowledge directors and knowledge officers – drawn, mostly, from the ranks of IT experts.

The principal source of the idea of 'knowledge work' is Peter Drucker. With typical farsightedness, he began to discuss the emergence of the knowledge worker as long ago as the 1960s.

Drucker's historical account argues that we have witnessed a dramatic shift in the way knowledge creates wealth. In the first part of the Industrial Revolution, knowledge was applied to tools, processes and products through the development of new technologies, patents and craft skills. Later, as industrialization and bureaucracy became more centralized, knowledge was applied to human work through work analysis and time-and-motion studies. Now, Drucker claims, productivity and competitive advantage depend on the application of knowledge to itself. Wealth creation in the 'knowledge society' depends on how well organizations can apply knowledge to existing knowledge. Success depends on the contribution of 'knowledge workers'.

Drucker's analysis has gained enormous credibility from the revolution in information technology. In some descriptions of the knowledge economy, knowledge is almost equated with technology. Knowledge becomes conflated with its own products, in a cumulative feedback loop between innovation and the uses of innovation. IT somehow captures the very productive forces that have created it and feeds human ingenuity back on itself in an ever more rapid spiral of innovation.

We should pause here. The urge to transform knowledge management into a technological project risks missing a vital point. Drucker is insistent that knowledge work is done by people, and that knowledge management is principally a matter of managing human relationships.

THE CHALLENGE OF MANAGING KNOWLEDGE WORKERS

Knowledge workers, according to Drucker's very broad definition, are workers whose main contribution is through their knowledge rather than manual labour. They are not defined merely by educational qualifications or professional status. For Drucker, anybody who contributes cognitively rather than manually qualifies.

More and more jobs, no matter what they are called, are taking on what Harvard academic Chris Argyris calls 'the contours of knowledge work'. The implications for operational managers are radical enough. How to define such work? How to account for knowledge in an organization's balance sheet? How to measure it? How best to reward it? How to get people to use their knowledge for the organization's benefit and – above all – share it? What sort of contractual relationships become necessary?

Knowledge workers' productivity is not easily measured. Drucker gives the simple example of the sales executive in the field. What is productivity for them?

> 'Is it total sales? Or is it the profit contribution from sales, which might vary tremendously with the product mix an individual sales-person sells? Or is it sales (or profit contribution) related to the potential of a sales territory? Perhaps a salesman's ability to hold old customers should be considered central to his productivity. Or perhaps it should be the ability to generate new accounts.'

The complexity of this analysis could easily be replicated for a host of knowledge workers.

The difficulties, however, go deeper than the challenge to traditional management accountancy. Drucker suggests that knowledge workers own and carry inside their heads an organization's primary means of production: knowledge. Their 'know-how' and 'know-what' constitute a form of personal 'equity'. Their knowledge gives them power; it makes them hard to control and eminently marketable. For this reason, perhaps, knowledge workers tend to see themselves as professionals rather than employees. They are more likely to be self-motivated than loyal. Indeed, they may feel uncomfortable in a traditional managerial culture stressing commitment to a collective enterprise, preferring the looser socializing culture of professional networks.

These are the people who will make innovation happen. Innovation is the ultimate in knowledge work: more than any other kind of work, innovation demands information, ideas, cognitive skills and creativity. Members of an innovation team are knowledge workers, virtually by definition.

Managing innovation, then, means managing knowledge workers as well as managing knowledge. Knowledge workers' effectiveness depends more on their expertise and problem-solving skills than on mechanical measures of efficiency.

But innovation demands more; they must also be able to *share* knowledge, to work in teams and on projects, to construct productive working relationships outside traditional managerial structures and to take responsibility for their own work.

CAPTURE AND RETRIEVAL – KNOWLEDGE MANAGEMENT AS MECHANICAL MEMORY

Knowledge management is commonly promoted as a means of codifying organizational memory. At its simplest, it is the process of documenting what people know before they take their knowledge 'out the door'.

Knowledge management thus becomes primarily a technical project. The growth of information technology promises the ability to store knowledge in unprecedented amounts, and to manipulate it with unprecedented sophistication. The knowledge stored can come from a host of sources, inside and outside the organization. Well structured, using intelligent search agents and engines, KM of this kind might prove invaluable in identifying opportunities for innovation.

Employees, of course, might view this benign project more darkly. Knowledge, after all, is power; capturing their knowledge is only a step away from appropriating it. Knowledge workers, in particular, might see KM as a conspiracy to disempower them and make them, literally, redundant.

Nonetheless, the simplification of KM into a technical project has proved extremely popular. It promises tangible benefits, outcomes that leaders can *see* on a screen or a spreadsheet. It gives managers the impression that they are taking control of knowledge. The emphasis on technological systems neatly sidesteps the awkward questions of how to encourage collaboration and creativity, how to motivate knowledge workers to share their knowledge, how to create a culture of trust and support for innovation. And there is undoubtedly a question of power: in the age of the powerful knowledge worker, IT-delivered knowledge management promises to hand power back to the organization.

Behind all this is a particular view of knowledge as a *thing*. 'Knowledge' – the noun – suggests that it is a resource that can be located, measured, extracted and used. The language of KM has become dominated by 'resource-based' metaphors. Information technology, we are told, provides the *tools* to *construct knowledge bases*, *knowledge webs* and *knowledge exchanges*. The aim of KM initiatives is to *stockpile* workers' knowledge (a dark military metaphor, this) and make it *accessible* through *search engines* and other *applications*. The metaphors of mining and drilling are common.

Viewing knowledge as a resource is self-evidently attractive. It fits neatly with the paradigm of an organization as an information-processing machine. Most leaders of organizations view their job precisely as managing quantifiable resources: processing 'raw' resources into products; exploiting those resources that add value, junking those that add cost.

This resource metaphor of knowledge has its uses. The notions of 'intellectual capital' or 'intellectual property', for example, have given new insights into the management of patents, licences and franchises. Many companies dependent on income from such properties have used IT with great success to manage their intellectual assets and derive more profit from them.

But a number of analysts and practitioners are beginning to notice that the resource-based approach to KM brings its own problems.

- **Not all knowledge can be codified.** Even if we were to separate 'know-what' from 'know-how', a good deal of what people know is not reducible to any language. The intuition that tells a sales executive when to press an advantage or leave alone, or suggests the cause of a tricky technical problem to an engineer, cannot easily be captured.

- **New information technologies don't in themselves guarantee improvements in performance.** Technology installed without the learning that enables people to use it may prove worthless, or worse.
- **People are not always willing to use new technology.** They may be unwilling to contribute information to it, to share it with others, to promote its existence or make it readily understandable. They may also be unwilling or unable to use the system.
- **Codifying knowledge into formal systems generates its own psychopathy.** The fluid, intuitive and informal practices that allow people and organizations to cope with uncertainty ossify into rigid structures that limit thinking.

All of these points are significant for innovation – but the last is especially important. Innovation demands thinking that transcends boundaries, that recognizes potential, that sees parallels between radically different activities or products, that translates images into productive ideas. A resource-based approach to knowledge management tends to inhibit the thinking that makes innovation possible.

KNOWLEDGE MANAGEMENT AND COLLABORATIVE LEARNING

Perhaps we should look at knowledge more as a means than an end. We might think of knowledge less as a resource to be exploited and more as a currency with which to create wealth. Knowledge is the medium by which we exchange and create new ideas. What matters is not so much how much knowledge we amass, as the way we *use* knowledge.

From the KM perspective, innovation might be defined as: *Sharing knowledge to create new products or services.*

Knowledge management, in this context, becomes the management of relationships. Collaboration is fundamental to innovation. Sharing knowledge is more than simply storing it and making it available. It requires us to concentrate on the way people relate to knowledge and codify it in language. It demands a sense of purpose to motivate people to share what they know. Above all, it means that we must encourage people to *create* knowledge collaboratively.

Our mechanistic view of organizations is not conducive to knowledge sharing. When work is segregated by function, organizations tend to develop 'silo' cultures in which different departments pursue their own objectives, constructing their own forms of knowledge in their own specialized language. Production may find it hard to talk to the finance department; the people in marketing may feel they can never get any sense out of the folk in product development; IT seem to live in a world of their own, and so on. Yet it is in the very interaction of these specialized forms of knowledge that the roots of innovation lie.

Innovation depends on sharing different types of knowledge. Analysts and practitioners have become increasingly aware over the last 20 years that innovation must include a learning dimension. KM, in this context, becomes the management of collaborative learning. Such learning is based in an understanding of human relationships. Any effort to promote innovation within an organization must take account of the way people learn, and how to help them learn together.

Part of the difficulty lies in working out what we mean by 'organizational learning'. First, most models of learning are behavioural, whereas our models of organizations tend to be mechanical. Organizations cannot think, let alone learn. Secondly, our models of learning tend to emphasize individual learning rather than collaborative learning. Thirdly, we tend – in the West, at least – to view learning as fundamentally rational. Where, after all, does learning take place? Most of us would probably answer 'in the mind'. We give little weight to practical learning or learning from experience: consider the difficulties practice-based qualifications have had in gaining recognition in the UK. We continue to value 'embrained' knowledge at the expense of other kinds of experience: the amassing of facts and the ability to rationalize rather than creativity, the acquisition of practical skills or the capacity for effective social action. Above all, our views of learning fundamentally inhibit our ability to share knowledge effectively. The kudos enjoyed by intellectual knowledge, gained at college, over practical knowledge gained at 'the school of hard knocks', often contributes to misunderstandings, resentment and jealousy between different departments or disciplines.

Learning is the process of creating new knowledge. It must involve both rational and experiential processes. And, if innovation means sharing what we know, then learning must involve learning collaboratively. Learning is as much about developing our skills in collaborative thinking, and doing, as about managing what we know.

CORPORATE FLOCKING AND SWAPPING – CREATING A FORUM FOR COLLABORATION AT THE LONDON BUSINESS SCHOOL

Companies might learn a thing or two from blue tits. Consider: both robins and blue tits have been known to learn how to pierce the foil tops of milk bottles. But robins are solitary birds; blue tits live and learn in flocks. Result: the tits beat the robins to the cream time and time again.

Flocking encourages innovation. To facilitate more corporate flocking, the London Business School and the Marketing Council have themselves flocked together to create Innovation Exchange, a network of companies keen to foster creativity and innovation by swapping ideas.

The Exchange was launched in 1999 by Stephen Byers, the UK's then Trade and Industry Secretary. It offers a leading collection of resource material, data, commercial information, practical advice and support relating to innovation across all fields. Everything is mediated by a website. For a subscription of £6,000 per year, companies can gain access to research, seminars and workshops – and a network of like-minded people.

Rob Goffee, Professor of Organizational Behaviour at London Business

School, says he wants to create a 'bring and buy' approach. 'We need to break down the barriers between companies, and between companies and business schools,' he says.

Companies on the membership list include big names like BAA, BT and Marks and Spencer. But is it realistic to expect competitors like Cadburys Schweppes and Mars – both currently members – to share ideas? 'That's for us to discover,' answers Goffee. 'The closer you get to patented R&D, the more cagey competitors are about sharing. The more you talk about management and ways of running businesses, the more people are willing to share.'

Interesting. Maybe that kind of tacit knowledge, fascinating as it is, is harder to steal.

RATIONALISM VS EMPIRICISM – THE ONGOING DEBATE

The conflict between intellectual learning and practical learning has ancient roots. In ancient Athens, a debate raged over the relative merits of empiricism and rationalism; the learning derived from experience and the learning derived from pure thought. Plato was the great advocate of rationalism, claiming that learning was the process of reasoning from axioms and theories. Mathematics is a classic example of rationalist thinking. Aristotle, on the other hand, was fiercely empirical. He claimed that we can derive knowledge only from sensory experience, and that the process of learning is the process of finding out by doing. Experimental science is empiricism at work. Rationalism deduces new knowledge from general principles; empiricism creates new knowledge inductively, deriving general truths from specific instances.

The split between rationalism and empiricism created a fundamental assumption that the essence of a human being is contained in a rational, thinking self, separate from what it experiences. We are isolated minds, either acting rationally on the world or being acted on by our empirical experiences. Descartes' famous saying 'I think, therefore I am' encapsulates the rationalist perspective. The empirical position is typified by John Locke, who asserts that none of our knowledge is innate, but that our minds at birth are like 'white paper' upon which experience 'writes' all our ideas.

A number of 20th century thinkers have attempted to heal the split between rationalism and empiricism by creating theories of *action*. What we know is determined by what we do: by our objectives, ambitions and priorities. Philosophers such as Husserl, Heidegger and Merleau-Ponty have sought to integrate the empirical and the rational by emphasizing the active relationship between the self and the outside world. Phenomenology, existentialism and some aspects of post-modernism relate what we learn more directly to what we *do*.

TACIT AND EXPLICIT KNOWLEDGE

Such philosophical ideas can find a sympathetic hearing in the 'can do' world of management. As a result, they increasingly have parallels in organizational theory. One of the best known examples is Michael Polanyi's distinction between *tacit* and *explicit* knowledge: terms that have a major part to play in KM.

Polanyi proposed, in 1966, that 'we can know more than we can tell'. Our knowledge is not merely what we have worked out rationally or learnt from textbooks. It includes what our bodies have learnt by acting in the world; our intuitions, the subtle interplay of hand and eye that guides us in a skilled activity. Explicit knowledge is what we can tell; it is knowledge codified into language and communicable. Explicit knowledge is contained in documents, instructions, graphs and any other medium that can be stored and transmitted. Tacit knowledge, on the other hand, is personal and context-specific. It is hard to formalize and communicate. It includes the hunches that tell us whether a customer is likely to buy a product, the complex juggling of variables that indicates a process may not be working right.

Polanyi suggests that tacit knowledge tends to be far more extensive than explicit knowledge. The knowledge that can be expressed in words and numbers is only the tip of the cognitive iceberg.

KOLB'S LEARNING CYCLE

The search is on, then, for a model of collaborative learning. Such a model should reconcile the rational and the empirical, and recognize the importance of both tacit and explicit knowledge. If we can understand the dynamics of collaborative learning more clearly, we may be able to develop a systematic approach to knowledge sharing in pursuit of innovation.

David Kolb's famous learning cycle is a good place to start the search: it is well known and is often used to manage learning programmes in organizations. Kolb published this model in 1974. He suggests that learning is a cycle in four stages.

FOUR STAGES OF LEARNING
1 **Concrete experience.**
2 **Reflection.**
3 **Conceptualization.**
4 **Experimentation.**

Learning begins with **experience**: we do something, or something happens to us. We then **reflect** upon the experience, asking what it means to us personally. On the basis of reflection, we **conceptualize**, deriving general rules from the experience or applying known theories to it. Our general concepts or theories then guide us to **experiment**, seeking to modify future experience. This cycle may happen in discrete steps, over a long period of time, or almost instantaneously.

Each step of the cycle produces different types of knowledge.

● Experience corresponds to what Kolb calls **'apprehension'** or knowledge by acquaintance. We might call it 'tacit knowledge'.

- Reflection transforms this knowledge through **'intension'**: the connotations we bring to the experience to locate it in our own structure of meaning. Reflection helps us to make tacit knowledge explicit by transforming it into language.
- Conceptualization manipulates explicit knowledge through language and generalizes meaning into universal theories. It transforms knowledge once again through **'comprehension'** (so called because our knowledge at this stage is more comprehensive than at other stages).
- Experimentation then tests the theory by **'extension'**: relating generalized knowledge back to experienced knowledge. Explicit knowledge, codified in language, is transformed once more into tacit knowledge.

Kolb's cycle thus reiterates, and seeks to integrate, the rational and empirical sides of learning. Experience is empirical and conceptualization rational; reflection and experimentation seek to mediate between the two.

Kolb further suggests that four different kinds of thinking are associated with each stage in the cycle.

FOUR KINDS OF THINKING

1 **Divergent thinking** (experience-reflection) generates multiple explanations of the same experience in an attempt to understand it more fully.
2 **Assimilative thinking** (reflection-conceptualization) sorts particular experiences into categories. It 'tidies up' our experience into structures of meaning. It works from particular instances to general truths.
3 **Convergent thinking** (conceptualization-experimentation) brings different facts and categories together with a single focus. Convergent thinking gives us answers and tells us whether they are right or wrong. Convergent thinking tells us what to do.
4 **Accommodative thinking** (experimentation-experience) shifts concepts, theories and categories in the light of particular experiences. It accommodates general truths to particular instances.

KOLB'S LEARNING CYCLE

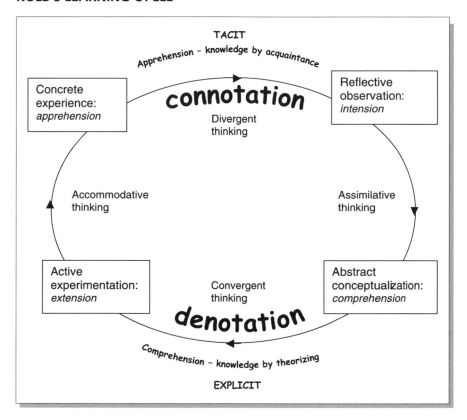

The dynamism of Kolb's model is its strongest feature. It suggests that learning is a multi-faceted activity, requiring both the messiness of empirical experience and the discipline of rational thought. The model may be limited, however, in the context of innovation. First, it is fundamentally individual in focus, with little to say about collaborative learning. Secondly, it tends to reinforce explicit knowledge at the expense of tacit.

We might explain this second limitation in terms of language. Reflecting on experience means making tacit knowledge explicit through language. Yet the language we choose limits the scope of our reflection to the terms we choose. It also determines how we theorize at the next stage of the cycle. The theories we construct – in language, of course – further determine the tests we carry out. Ultimately, they limit the experience that follows. The cycle reinforces the structures of meaning we adopt, even in adapting them. As a result, we tend to limit our enquiry. Language forces us to focus and refine our experience rather than expand and enrich it. Other tacit areas of knowledge become increasingly unavailable to us.

Kolb's cycle probably works best, therefore, as a model of *adaptive* learning: improving a skill or a process, for example. Innovation, though, requires a more radical approach: not individual but collaborative; not adaptive but generative.

CHRIS ARGYRIS AND DOUBLE-LOOP LEARNING

Chris Argyris developed the idea of 'double-loop learning' in an attempt to break this limiting cycle. Argyris has spent over 20 years examining conscious and unconscious reasoning processes. He asserts that we hold maps in our heads about how to plan, implement and review our actions. Few of us are aware that the maps we use are *not* the theories we might explicitly offer to explain our actions. Even fewer are aware of the maps or theories we do use. Argyris proposes that we all use two theories to explain our actions: a theory consis-

---

ESPOUSED THEORY AND THEORY-IN-USE – AN EXAMPLE

When asked how he would deal with a disagreement with a member of his team, a project leader answered that he would first state his understanding of the disagreement then negotiate what kind of data he and the team member could agree would resolve it. This represents his espoused theory (or the theory behind what he says): joint control of the problem. A tape recording of the leader in such a situation, however, revealed that he actually advocated his own point of view and dismissed the team member's. This indicated his theory-in-use (or the theory behind what he did).

tent with what we say, and another consistent with what we do. Our **espoused theory** is the world view and values we believe underpin our behaviour. Our **theory-in-use** is our actual world view and values, implied by our behaviour. The two theories often fail to match.

Argyris suggests that nothing we do is accidental. We *design* our actions, even though we may be unaware that we are doing so, or that our design is different from the one we *think* we are using.

How, then, can we manage our behaviour more effectively? Argyris suggests that we should work towards greater congruence between these two theories.

THEORY-IN-USE – KEY ELEMENTS

Argyris' model contains a number of elements that help to explain how we link our thoughts and actions. **Governing values** are beliefs that we try to maintain by our actions. We all have many governing values. Our

---

THEORY-IN-USE – AN EXAMPLE

A member of an innovation project team may have a **governing value** of suppressing conflict, and another of being competent. In any given situation, she will design **action strategies** to keep both these governing values intact. For instance, faced with conflict, she might say as little as possible. This may (she hopes) suppress the conflict, yet allow her to appear competent – because at least she hasn't said anything wrong. This strategy will have various **consequences**, both for her and the others involved. An **intended consequence** might be that the other parties will eventually give up the discussion, thereby successfully suppressing the conflict. As she has said little, she may feel she has not left herself open to being seen as incompetent. An **unintended consequence** might be that she thinks the situation has been left unresolved and therefore likely to recur, and feels dissatisfied.

actions are likely to affect any number of them, and any situation may trigger a trade-off between them. **Action strategies** are what we do to keep our governing values intact. These strategies will have **consequences** that are both **intended** – those we believe will result – and **unintended**.

When the consequences of an action strategy are what we want, then intention and outcome match and our theory-in-use is confirmed. However, the consequences of an action strategy may be unintended and counterproductive. In this case, there is a mismatch between intention and outcome.

Argyris suggests that we can respond in two ways to this mismatch. He labels these responses single and double-loop learning.

SINGLE-LOOP AND DOUBLE-LOOP LEARNING

The first response to a mismatch between intention and outcome is to search for another strategy that will satisfy the governing value. For example, we might have a governing value of improved packing rates on a production line, and another of personal competence in managing the line. An action strategy might be to criticize packers for wasting time and suggest they get on with the task at hand. This may indeed improve productivity and create a feeling of personal competence: the fault has been laid at someone else's feet. The change is in the action, not in the governing value. This is **single-loop learning**.

Another possible response would be to challenge the governing values themselves. For example, we might examine the value of improved productivity in the context of overall work patterns, or quality control. We might even challenge our own view that our competence is directly implicated in the actions of the packers. The result of this enquiry might be to review shift patterns or worker responsibilities, or to delegate responsibility for some aspects of productivity to a team leader. Old governing values might be discarded and new ones substituted. In this case, both the action strategy and the governing value have changed. This is **double-loop learning**.

Double-loop learning might help us to break down the 'defensive routines' that inhibit knowledge sharing. Defensive routines are action strategies that seek to maintain the *status quo* in the face of threat or change, by blinding us to the very existence of that change. Such defensive routines are deadly enemies of innovation.

CREATING KNOWLEDGE – NONAKA AND TAKEUCHI

In 1995, Ikujiro Nonaka and Hirotaka Takeuchi published *The Knowledge-creating Company*. It has become a seminal text in knowledge management. Nonaka and Takeuchi offer the beginnings of a coherent theory of KM for innovation, incorporating well developed ideas of learning.

For Nonaka and Takeuchi, innovation is always the aim of the exercise. Managing knowledge is a means to a creative end, not a self-justifying project. In a striking summary of their position, they highlight the distinction we have already seen several times, between operational or functional work and innovative work. They criticize the view of organizations as mechanisms for processing resources into predictable outputs:

> 'Although this view has proven to be effective in explaining how organizations function, it has a fundamental limitation. From our perspective, it does not really explain innovation. When organizations innovate, they do not simply process information, from the outside in, in order to solve existing problems and adapt to a changing environment. They actually create new knowledge and information, from the inside out, in order to redefine both problems and solutions and, in the process, to re-create their environment.'

Operational work seeks to optimize the processes and functions that already exist in an organization. Kolb's single-loop learning cycle adequately explains the adaptive learning necessary to maintain this operational cycle. Innovation is a different kind of work and it must be organized differently. It also requires a different kind of learning: generative learning, which explores reality for multiple experiences and generates new knowledge through collaborative interaction.

Nonaka and Takeuchi start with Polanyi's distinction between tacit and explicit knowledge.

- They see **tacit knowledge** as what we learn through involvement with the world. It is subjective, bodily knowledge of the here and now; knowledge by practical acquaintance. It includes our mental models: the paradigms, perspectives and beliefs that guide our actions. It includes, too, our action knowledge: our skills, crafts and know-how. Crucially, tacit knowledge also includes our feelings, our hopes, wishes, dreams and ambitions.
- **Explicit knowledge**, in contrast, is what we learn through language or discourse. It is 'book learning': objective, rational, theoretical knowledge of universal truths, applicable not just in the here and now but also in the 'there and then'. Explicit knowledge is the 'know-what' that complements our know-how. It can be codified and recorded.

Nonaka and Takeuchi stress that these two modes of knowing are partners; they interact with, and change into, each other in our creative activities. They are transformed into each other socially, through four processes of what the writers call 'knowledge conversion'.

- **Socialization** (tacit to tacit) is the process of sharing experiences. It is the form of learning typified by apprenticeship or on-the-job training, in which mental models and technical skills are 'absorbed' by shared experience.
- **Externalization** (tacit to explicit) is the process of articulating tacit knowledge into explicit concepts. Nonaka and Takeuchi call this 'the quintessential knowledge-creation process' because it is through externalization that private thinking can be shared with others without the need to share an experience. The simplest example of externalization would be documenting a process; writing is the art of converting tacit knowledge into explicit information. But externalization can take other

forms: metaphor, imagery, hypotheses, analogies and models all help to externalize. Externalization is triggered by reflection and dialogue.

- **Combination** (explicit to explicit) is the process of systematizing concepts into knowledge systems. Documents, meetings, networks and databases all help to combine different bodies of explicit knowledge. Corporate visions, business or product concepts and customer service management systems are all business outcomes of combination.
- **Internalization** (explicit to tacit) is the process of embodying explicit knowledge into 'unconscious competence' or a body of values. Learning by doing is a good way to internalize knowledge. Documentation is helpful, as is the 'story telling' that helps to internalize corporate values through emotional involvement.

Nonaka and Takeuchi integrate these four modes of knowledge conversion into a five-phase model of 'organizational knowledge creation'. These five phases – sharing tacit knowledge, creating concepts, justifying concepts, building an archetype and 'cross-levelling of knowledge' – are effectively a KM strategy to support innovation.

- **Sharing tacit knowledge.** Tacit knowledge is only ever held by individuals. For it to become socialized within the organization, a 'field' must be created in which people can interact through dialogue of various kinds. Here, suggest Nonaka and Takeuchi, 'people share experiences and synchronize their bodily and mental rhythms'. A typical such field would be a self-organizing team gathered to initiate an innovation project, discussing what the brief might mean, how their different experiences might help them reflect differently on it and setting the task boundaries of the project.
- **Creating concepts.** Once the team has started to share mental models, it articulates it through words and ideas, externalizing the idea in all sorts of ways: deduction, induction, dialectics, metaphor and analogy. This stage is crucial to the innovation process, because it is here that the team can diverge their thinking to create multiple concepts and new ideas, and act together to create a 'knowledge spiral'. It is in

the interaction of tacit and explicit knowledge that innovation is born; the knowledge spiral is a model of how that process might work.

● **Justifying concepts.** At this stage, concepts are refined so they can be judged as to their suitability for the organization and its strategy. This stage involves screening, both quantitatively and qualitatively.

● **Building an archetype.** The justified concept is converted into something tangible: a prototype or a pilot. This is combined with existing knowledge in the organization to find out how well it might work – within the organization and with the organization's customers. Attention to detail now becomes critically important.

● **Cross-levelling of knowledge.** The knowledge creation that produced the innovation moves onto a new level. Knowledge that has become an innovation within the company may trigger new ideas in other parts of the organization, or stimulate interest and knowledge creation among the organization's suppliers, partners or customers. Knowledge creation continues, spiralling out from the project into its environment in a never-ending process.

The similarities with Kolb's learning cycle are indeed striking. We could tentatively map the stages of one cycle onto the other.

Kolb's learning cycle	Modes of knowledge transformation	Organizational knowledge creation
• Concrete experience	• Socialization	• Sharing tacit knowledge
• Reflection	• Externalization	• Creating concepts
• Conceptualization	• Combination	• Justifying concepts
		• Building an archetype
• Experimentation	• Internalization	• Cross-levelling of knowledge

The key difference is Nonaka and Takeuchi's emphasis on social action rather than individual learning. This is properly a model of organizational learning, and of generative rather than adaptive learning. Rather than creating an internal focus on improving a single activity, the focus of this model is outwards: knowledge creation fuelling more and yet more knowledge creation at different levels of the organization. Nonaka and Takeuchi use a striking image to capture this outward focus:

> 'We call this the "knowledge spiral", in which the interaction between tacit knowledge and explicit knowledge will become larger in scale as it moves up the ontological levels. Thus, organizational knowledge creation is a spiral process, starting at the individual level and moving up through expanding communities of interaction that cross sectional, departmental, divisional and organizational boundaries.'

Nonaka and Takeuchi take the concept of knowledge management onto a new level of sophistication. Rather than being simply a means of creating organizational memory, they see KM as the process of facilitating organizational knowledge creation; organizational learning in all but name. And all in the pursuit of innovation, which is throughout their book the fundamental reason for engaging in knowledge creation.

Any knowledge management initiative must seek to integrate the explicit knowledge contained in systems and databases with the tacit knowledge contained in people's heads and hearts. An IT-based approach will emphasize:

- systems;
- networks; and
- processes of knowledge conversion (through documenting procedures or customer statistics, for example).

We must balance this approach with another, more humanistic, approach that emphasizes:

- business processes;
- customer relationships;
- teamworking;
- career management; and
- reward systems.

Getting knowledge workers to share what they know and learn collaboratively may be the greatest challenge for any organization seeking to innovate. We might start, not by reorganizing the architecture of our information infrastructure, but by reassessing the contracts we make with knowledge workers. Perhaps we should start to see them as an investment, rather than a cost. After all, technologies grow obsolete; people have the limitless potential to create knowledge throughout their working lives. Their contribution in the knowledge era represents a directly productive force; they can increase efficiency through their ability to reorganize production and design; and, of course, unlike computers, they can innovate.

Creating water wizards – are wise people the best innovators?

PETER MATTHEWS

Peter Matthews has worked in the water industry for 40 years. He was the UK's first director of innovation and is a leading expert on knowledge management. He was Deputy Managing Director of Anglian Water International until July 1999 and is now Chairman of Pelican Portfolio, an independent consultancy.

Water utilities have been managing knowledge for years – although they may not have always known it! Sweeping changes in the industry over the last 20 years, however, have profoundly altered the way the industry thinks about knowledge, and manages it.

In 1974, regional water authorities were established in the UK, based on river catchments. Hundreds of small operations were amalgamated into regional management, with a new philosophy transcending that of municipalities. Regional knowledge bases had to be established in order to migrate best practice. However, these authorities were still constrained by non-commercial rules and were purely UK operations. In 1989, the 'big bang' occurred: water companies had to transform themselves from public authorities into global companies (in some cases they remained as UK companies). At the forefront of this transformation was Anglian Water – the company for which I worked, and in which I helped to develop a new approach to knowledge management. Our experience has provided a conceptual framework that may be of interest to other organizations.

THE CHANGE DRIVERS

Faced with the seismic change of privatization, Anglian had to adapt, grow and improve – all at the same time. We had to:

- respond to a new commercial environment with shareholders;
- increase the levels of service with a focus on customers;
- improve cost efficiencies, knowing that water charges would have to rise to finance a massive capital investment programme;
- grow the business, particularly in overseas markets.

Such specific needs were expressions of the same fundamental need: to become smarter. And the only way to become smarter was to become more learned. After all, happy, committed, learned employees are more flexible and more productive than unhappy, uncommitted, ignorant employees. At the crux of this wave of change in Anglian was a unique institution: The University of Water.

The leadership of the company initiated a massive change programme in 1993. Through experiences such as a period at Harvard Business School, we had realized that this programme had to be radically different. It had to be innovation in its broadest sense. Although some leaders have gone, that drive from the top has continued to the present.

We began with a strategic review in 1993/4 and set to work re-engineering our business processes. The results of the review were implemented through a total quality management (TQM) programme: the company adopted the principles of the European Foundation for Quality Management and became a 'registered' learning organization in late 1994. Training had been turning into learning, however, since 1989. Previously, although craft and professional employees had had training, little had been available for front-line operational staff. Learning now includes understanding the 'why' as well as the 'how' about work, in personal, team, group and social contexts. It has broadened, too, to include all employees.

'Executive Stretch' programmes began at the top of the organization and then became a firm-wide programme called the 'Transformation Journey'.

This was an open learning process, designed to encourage more nimble, open thinking. It consisted of a three-stage, two-year programme of self-awareness learning and project work.

The vision of innovation as a business process that emerged from these programmes drew together a range of organizational functions and processes, including:

- conventional research and development;
- business change library services; and
- knowledge management suggestion schemes.

THE UNIVERSITY OF WATER – A NEW VISION

Groups of people who had made the Transformation Journey helped to give birth to the idea of a corporate university. Thus, the corporate university was born out of the very process of innovation to which it contributes.

We registered our new federal learning organization, the University of Water, in 1994. (We had to register the name Aqua Universitas rather than University of Water, for legal reasons. I shall refer to it as the University of Water from now on as its working title.) Anglian Water is not the first international organization to develop these ideas, but it is the first in the water sector. Motorola University is a well known example from the electronics and telecommunications sector.

The corporate university is a mechanism for delivering a learning organization and knowledge management. The principal objectives of a corporate university should be to:

- create learning environments that actively promote learning;
- promote knowledge creation;
- link learning to business needs, development and plans;
- measure learning processes and results;
- enable external partners, particularly universities, to join in;
- create a company-wide learning organization and local learning envi-

ronments that reflect local needs and, more crucially, that individuals can relate to;

- permit a diversity of learning environments to allow different cultural requirements to be included in group needs;
- exploit the intellectual advantage of the concepts behind the university;
- promote employability rather than employment.

A corporate university embraces a number of paradoxes. For example, we might distinguish 'soft' learning and cultural activities from 'hard' training in business activities; yet they are inextricably linked. We might distinguish individual learning from corporate learning. Learning is focused on personal development; yet, ultimately, the company benefits with better employees and higher profits. Personal, team and organizational learning are all part of the same process. A further paradox is the uneasy balance between a desire for freedom and the need for stable structures: freedom to develop from experience through empowerment and structure in 'the way we do things around here' to ensure consistency.

The university is the whole company. It exists in the hearts and minds of employees. But there is a need to have some tangible assets, to satisfy the need to 'touch and feel' the university. A sense of ownership by all employees is crucial. The university has as its vision the aim to create and spread knowledge for sustainable water management. It thus mitigates against both knowledge anorexia and knowledge hoarding: the 'Scrooge effect' in which individuals withhold knowledge for personal power.

CREATIVITY, INNOVATION AND KNOWLEDGE – THE BASIC PRINCIPLES

The University of Water helps the Anglian group to have the best people, the best teams and the best organization to provide the best service – through wisdom, creation and exploitation. Some academics might say that wisdom and creativity are not connected; our experience is different.

Creativity provides the essential spirit and behaviour from which innovation and tangible beneficial change take place. Innovation is the wise exploitation of creativity. The very essence of creativity and innovation is the creation and spread of knowledge – which is itself linked to wisdom.

These form part of an interconnected process which we can represent linearly.

Data   >   Information   >   Knowledge   >   Wisdom
or experience

The relationship of creativity and wisdom has been recognized by many ancient traditions. For Christians, Jews and Muslims, the wisdom of God is the power by which He created the universe, which is itself the first delight of God. This notion is also well known to Asian cultures. These ancient teachings suggest that the relationship between creativity, knowledge and wisdom is cyclical, rather than linear. Creativity lies beyond wisdom but feeds back into knowledge.

In their book *The Knowledge-creating Company*, Nonaka and Takeuchi recognize that knowledge creation leads to continuous innovation. If we search for a new concept for the combination of innovation and knowledge management, which is an evolutionary step, the words 'kennovation' and 'kennovating' seem appropriate ('ken' is an old English word meaning understanding). A kennovation model is given below. This is, in effect, a learning loop: knowledge applied to create innovation, which itself leads to new knowledge, fuelling yet further innovation.

THE KENNOVATION CYCLE

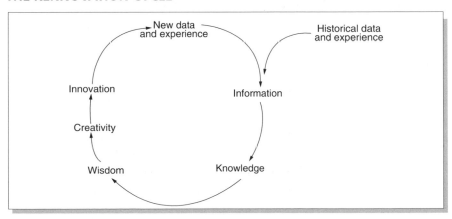

Where should 'understanding' sit within this model? Should we interpose it between 'knowledge' and 'wisdom'? Or is it an essential ingredient of each of them? Indeed, I am not really clear if Nonaka and Takeuchi envisaged wisdom as being contained within knowledge. However, I think that it is worth making a distinction between wisdom and knowledge. Wisdom is the critical ability to use knowledge in a constructive way. Equally, wisdom has in it the critical ability to discern ways in which new ideas can be created.

Knowledge from new sources has greatest value when combined with knowledge from established sources. This idea can be developed further. If knowledge and innovation do interact cyclically, how does an organization avoid going round and round in pointless circles? How can it represent itself as moving forward? One way is to use a helix as shown in the diagram below. This is an example of a learning spiral referred to in Nonaka and Takeuchi's book.

KENNOVATION HELIX

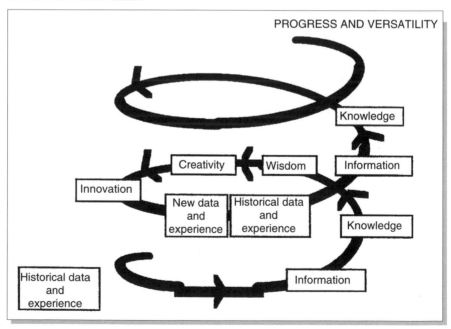

The 'Kennovation Helix' is an example of double-loop learning, which is in itself a learning spiral. So learning about learning has been a very important driver in organizational evolution.

EXPLOITING THE WISDOM OF MATURITY

We must capture wisdom as part of innovation throughout an organization's business processes. Innovation is not all about the new and the young. Experienced people can contribute in constructive ways. Maybe there is a place in innovation for remarks such as 'We tried this before and it didn't work then' – provided that such a contribution is driven not by a sense of failure or protectionism, but by an insight into the opportunities and options remaining for the future. Wisdom helps to define the size of the three envelopes of empowerment – 'Get on without reference back', 'You may find it useful to refer back', and 'You get approval before you proceed'.

Western society forgets the wisdom of the past – and of the East – by not exploiting the creativity of maturity. Maybe we should match that old expression 'You can't teach an old dog new tricks' with 'You can teach a new dog old tricks', and even, 'An old dog can teach old tricks'! It may well be that an old dog can discover new tricks. Wisdom is not necessarily restricted to old people and creativity is not necessarily restricted to young people.

The role of a mentor is critical in passing on both wisdom and encouraging self-expression. Mentoring can be related to personal advice on careers, a retained expertise, specific courses, and so on.

How do these competencies – creativity and wisdom – relate to each other? For example, can a person be creative without necessarily being wise and *vice versa*? This depends to some extent on how we define the concepts. Is there a distinction between intellectual creativity and artistic creativity? Are artists wise people? A lot of painters and poets have shown a distinct lack of wisdom or innovation in exploiting their creativity. On the other hand, many engineers are intellectually creative: for them, some psychometrics are difficult to complete – painting a sunset or designing a bridge may be more pleasurable experiences. What activity did Leonardo da Vinci enjoy most?

The essence of the relationship between creativity and wisdom is that the experience and judgement of wisdom enables creativity to have a focus and direction. So does intellectual creativity arise out of wisdom or is it a complementary characteristic, which by synergy, facilitates a move forward? As far as the Kennovation Helix is concerned, it may not be relevant to the end result, but it is important in determining how an organization is to develop itself.

THE NEED FOR WISDOM AND INNOVATION IN THE WATER INDUSTRY

Changes in utility industries have demonstrated that these ideas are far from irrelevant. British utilities have faced political and economic changes that are being repeated around the world.

It is often said that crisis precipitates change. IBM is an oft-quoted example. The trauma and catharsis of a change such as privatization does create the right stimulus for organizational and cultural change. But the real trick is to get utility employees to see that they need to change *without* the drama of a crisis.

The process of change is a managed paradox. On one hand, there are demands for greater public involvement, greater employee involvement and support, and greater environmental investment. On the other hand, there are demands for less cost, less bureaucracy, less peripheral activity, a clearer focus on business objectives – and fewer employees.

This paradox is best managed if the organization is versatile. It must be flexible, able to cope with circumstances as they occur as well as plan ahead rigorously. So the end result of wisdom creation is versatility. Anglian Water is destined to become a prime example of a *versatile organization,* in which the stability of public service is matched with the change capability of entrepreneurial business. A versatile organization will show a positive correlation between wisdom and creativity.

We can express the relationship of creativity and wisdom in a Boston square diagram.

RELATIONSHIP OF WISDOM AND CREATIVITY

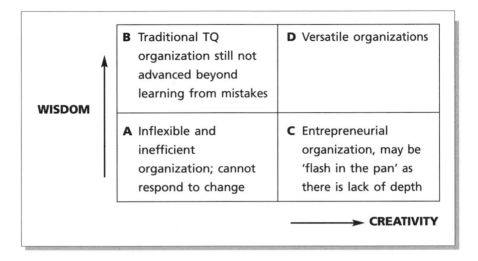

The water utilities, like Anglian Water, will continue as laboratories of change in the 21st century. We will need to create and use wisdom in making these changes, by becoming versatile.

It is vital for a water utility to get its culture right. It must balance the needs of the organization and of its employees with the technology it employs for the benefit of external stakeholders. It will need the Kennovation Helix to do so. The wisdom of the organization will also allow the needs of the external stakeholders to be balanced: customers, regulators, environment, shareholders, and so on. Managing the needs of those stakeholders means that better services have to be provided at less cost – which means smarter people, smarter processes and smarter technology.

The provision of water is a sensitive matter within communities. The debate is not only about public service vs profit – which can be combined satisfactorily and beneficially. The way we manage water expresses something about the very spirit of a society. The earliest civilizations arose around the need to co-operate for the provision of irrigation water. Catchment management and the provision of community water services are social paradigms for co-operation and trust. The providers of water are more than just shopkeepers; they do serve a higher purpose and their behaviour is judged in this context.

We can lead the way in social transformation by behaving in ways that demonstrate these higher principles – ways that are wise and creative.

RUNNING THE UNIVERSITY OF WATER

The University of Water has a federal structure. We developed our own university with its own structural syntax within Anglian Water Services, drawn from the structural models of traditional universities. However, people from other parts of the group were involved and it is intended that, when Anglian has sufficient experience, the practices will be extended throughout the whole.

A learning council advises the executive team on the Anglian Water brand of learning. The council consists of learners from all parts of the company. Its objectives include meeting the group's overall aspiration and using a learning culture to develop its business activities. These objectives embrace the minimum acceptable achievement and rate of progress for all learning activities within the group. The council provides a central focus for audit feedback and high level business synergies through learning. More broadly, it seeks to resolve the paradox of encouraging the freedom to develop from experience through empowerment while maintaining a structured set of consistent processes.

Each of the companies within the group is responsible for developing a local learning organization or community. In the case of Anglian Water Services, the learning organization is sub-divided into business unit processes. Each business unit has a learning champion. Such a structure will permit unique needs to be satisfied, and also encourage experiment, local ownership of learning and teamwork. The results of each experiment must be migrated to other business units in shared best practices. However, some formal mechanisms are needed to strengthen cross-process and organizational learning.

In 1994, the company established a series of networks to exchange knowledge and share best practice across the group. Examples were executive management networks, technology networks and learning networks. In the latter cases, individuals are free to join and even establish new ones. The networks may be temporary or permanent and address issues of general or specific interest. These networks provided the insight for the next step in the evolution of the university. Several of these are what we called 'catalysed networks'. The organization sets up an initial team by invitation around a key topic with a facilitator, and then leaves it to evolve as it wishes. Catalysed networks have been drivers of success in technology innovation, drawing on all parts of the group.

These networks perform a vital role in transforming knowledge throughout the company.

Any knowledge-creating organization – like the one Anglian Water is aspiring to become – must evolve to be able to acquire, create, exploit and accumulate new knowledge, continuously and repeatedly. A hierarchical, formally structured organization carries out this task mainly by combination and internalization. Self-organizing teams in networks, as part of an overall learning process, perform the task by socialization and externalization.

The organization is in the process of establishing company colleges as knowledge networks. In 1996, three colleges were started, based on the topics of creativity, open learning and international learning. These would have the dual purpose of promoting organizational learning and encouraging personal learning. They would provide a focal point for cross-company activities but would not become isolated. So, for example, people from throughout the world working for Anglian Water could still participate in the technology networks.

The College of International Learning was set up to facilitate the University of Water's participation in the world wide web of learning. It would act as a focal point for an international scholarship programme and ensure that operational visitors were dealt with on a structured, rather than an *ad hoc*, basis. The colleges would have a wide range of learning styles – the intention was to have individual learning (books, computer programmes, etc), small groups, mentoring and wide communities. The university as a whole is an example of 'rainbow learning'.

Different models can be used as benchmarks for this federal concept. We based our vision on the structure of an academic university: the local learning organizations are analogous to departments, and the knowledge networks to colleges.

Another useful model is provided by the large pre-planned cities that are being created in many places in the world. The city has an overall identity, but there are suburbs or city villages with their own local identities and communities. Similarly, the University of Water has a distinct identity, and the learning networks and colleges have their own identities and communities of practice.

STRUCTURING KNOWLEDGE IN THE ORGANIZATION

By summer 1997, a number of major steps had been taken to address the issue of what knowledge was actually needed in the business.

Three 'layers' of knowledge management were established.

THREE LAYERS OF KNOWLEDGE

1 At the bottom of the organization is the knowledge base 'layer', embracing tacit knowledge – associated with organizational culture and procedures – as well as explicit knowledge in the form of documents, filing systems and computerized databases. This archival layer is in effect the primary means of facilitating change, renewing the knowledge base and supporting learning.

2 The second layer is the 'business system', production and customer services in Anglian Water, where normal routine operations are carried out.

3 The top layer is an area where multiple self-organizing teams create knowledge. These teams share in the joint creation of knowledge.

The knowledge base layer containing a number of core knowledge areas can give new insights into core competencies and the way they can be developed. It contains the knowledge assets of the company.

Some examples of knowledge assets for Anglian Water might be:

Fundamental	**Social**	**Applied**
Biology	Fiscal/economics	Ecology
Physics	Socio-politics	Construction engineering
Chemistry	Psychology	Education
	Sociology	
	IT	
	Cybersciences	

These knowledge assets may be combined in knowledge application systems; the extent and depth of the combinations will depend on what is needed by the business. For example, if an activity is outsourced, Anglian's knowledge of the outsourced system will be diminished but will have to be supplemented by an ability to manage the outsourced contract. Knowledge application systems include fluid distribution systems (combination of physics and construction engineering), environmental management (ecology, fiscal/economics and socio-politics) and capital management (IT, construction engineering, fiscal/economics).

Clearly, this approach opens up a debate as to what core knowledge areas are essential for running the business. The core knowledge application systems may be converted into business activities by subjecting them to exploitation criteria which the business may wish to accept for its future development. This provides a much more structured, knowledge-based approach to the contentious debate on core competencies and outsourcing. This is shown diagramatically overleaf. The structure of this diagram is inspired by the structure of scientific domains outlined by Kao, a Japanese manufacturing company, and illustrated in Nonaka and Takeuchi's book.

ANGLIAN WATER'S KNOWLEDGE DOMAINS

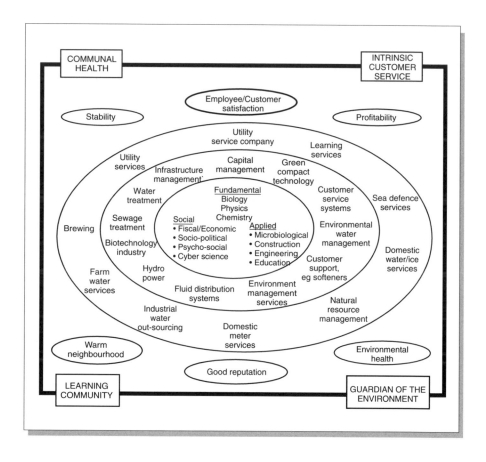

The company is already looking at some of the business opportunities arising out of analysis described in the knowledge domains diagram above.

At the same time, the directors identified the key capabilities considered to be necessary for success and for which knowledge will have to be sustained and enhanced. So the concepts of knowledge and capability were joined together.

The core knowledge areas became four faculties: Engineering and Technology, Humanities and Social Sciences, Business Development and Management, and Environment and Planning. The colleges are mechanisms to take forward the key capabilities grouped within the faculties.

We now believe that knowledge creation should be added as a faculty.

Faculties (Deans)	Key Capabilities/College
1 Engineering and Technology	Pipeline management Operating treatment works Project management Waste/water treatment (treatment technology)
2 Humanities and Social Sciences	Customer service Change management Anglian brand
3 Business Development and Management	Negotiating and managing contracts Product offering and development Asset management
4 Environment and Planning	Water resource management Water quality Economic regulation

More progress is being made with the more 'tangible' colleges such as the Colleges of Treatment Technology, Project Management and Water Quality. This is not surprising when one remembers Anglian Water's origins and business needs. The Colleges of Creativity and Open Learning are being dissolved: henceforth, each faculty will be responsible for ensuring that it promotes creativity and uses the facilities of the open learning network. Each faculty has a lead team to co-ordinate and support the faculty's overall direction. They are headed by senior directors. Each college is headed by a director or senior manager.

A small permanent team develops the university and supports the faculties and colleges. It is inspiring to see these people at work, particularly as two of the team were recruited through the Transformation Journey from the operational front-line. They have been working on developing a 'Mastery of Best Practice' initiative, which will embrace a number of Anglian's learning initiatives and recognize the egalitarian vision of 'fitfor-purpose learning'. They are also working on accreditation with a number of universities.

The idea of a portfolio of roles is beginning to emerge from these experiences. An individual has what we traditionally know as 'day job responsibilities', but now also has a number of university responsibilities. This is causing some concerns about the balance of time spent on these activities – particularly in an organization which is striving to become more efficient in the day job. So, there has to be a balance between effort spent on the present and planning for the future, and between the local unit needs and the greater good of the group.

Efforts are being made to quantify how much resource the company can afford for learning and change. This should be assessed as part of the annual business planning process.

CREATING A VIRTUAL CAMPUS

Any self-respecting university should have a campus. Where should Anglian's be? The company had been developing a training centre at Whitwell in central England for many years. This has been a physical focus for the Transformation Journey and the University of Water team. However, we were loathe to make Whitwell the campus of the university because it could become perceived as just 'something else in training' provided by human resources (Whitwell is currently part of HR).

Instead, we established a virtual campus on the intranet. The idea of 'HAWK' (Harnessing Anglian Water's Knowledge) was born when we realized that tacit, and even explicit, knowledge was being lost as the years progressed and people left. So we started with the Encyclopaedia of Water to capture this knowledge. The encyclopaedia is now one site on the virtual campus, along with manuals and home pages on special topics. HAWK is where learning is available. Courses can be divided into the knowledge areas represented in the faculties, which then have a role in determining the direction of learning for people's needs.

The intranet and university are now managed by the same central team (the system for the intranet is managed by CSC, the outsource partner for computing in Anglian Water).

Anglian's unique approach is a real step forward in combining personal and organizational learning.

MANAGING THE INNOVATION PROCESS

The Innovation Directorate was founded as one of the innovative changes in 1994. It was the first such directorate in any company in the UK. Its purpose was to develop technological innovation and stimulate organizational innovation. There was an early debate as to whether having a separate process (a synonym for directorate or department in Anglian Water) would inhibit the process of innovation throughout the business. People might assume 'I don't have to be innovative – that's the job of the innovation department!' However, the alternative view was that such a directorate would provide a role model and source of energetic catalysis within the group – and so, indeed, it proved.

The directorate amalgamated four existing functions: R&D, the library, Anglian's suggestion scheme and the business change unit. It aimed to provide intelligence to develop and exploit new technologies in internal and external business settings, and to stimulate positive changes in business practice.

Including the suggestion scheme in this initiative proved interesting. We discovered that we needed to manage ideas in just the same way that we exploit new technologies. Bright ideas need to be evaluated, developed and marketed, even internally. We appreciated early on that marketing was a very closely aligned process and the innovation directorate took a strong lead in technical marketing. In fact, as we shall see later, the concept emerged of research and marketing, with development becoming implicit in the function.

One initiative quickly led to others. For example, manual operators were given secondment opportunities. The benefits were twofold: it demonstrated the group's new egalitarian culture and reduced the perceived and real remoteness of researchers. Other initiatives included establishing HAWK, the company intranet and an early site on the internet. Out of the Innovation Directorate grew the knowledge creation process and leadership in the University of Water. These are now standalone processes.

FROM RESEARCH AND DEVELOPMENT TO RESEARCH AND MARKETING

These initiatives led us to realize that research had to become more outward looking.

We noticed that traditional R&D tended to be rather introverted, self-serving and isolated from the rest of the business. On the other hand, we recognized that not all research can produce successful products, processes and services. Indeed, there is a strong argument for saying that there should be a significant element of entrepreneurial risk taking within the R&D process. Safe research will not necessarily lead to 'quantum breakthroughs'.

The Innovation Directorate is now much more extrovert than traditional R&D: more outward looking and locked into the needs of the rest of the organization. It is probably more appropriate to think of innovation as being part of research and marketing rather than research and development.

Anglian Water has distilled a vision for the development of its technology. They see themselves leading the way to the future with green, clean, compact technology that costs less to use and own. This vision informs their practice globally and as a complete organization. Any organization using technology that is environmentally unfriendly is unlikely to be focused on its environment or its customers' needs. So the nature of the technology provides a view of how the company deals with its customers and how it behaves in general.

This vision has led to new ways of thinking and behaving. Anglian have learnt that the needs of the market must drive technological innovation. Technologists within the innovation process have become responsible for encouraging creativity within the wider organization. They must also now help to market new technologies, launch processes successfully and support them fully once they succeed in the marketplace. Anglian have established a strengthening network between innovation technologists and colleagues responsible for technical marketing elsewhere in the group. This is proving to be very successful in determining the direction of both research and marketing.

This new approach has led to some innovative ideas in marketing. The processes available for exploitation are now launched annually as a designer range of green, clean compact technologies. The concepts are based on those used by other industries such as the car industry. They contain components that are the established models, slightly updated 'models', brand new 'models' and concepts with tantalizing hints of things to come. Each technology is given a persona which customers can relate to. For example, the new range of compact sewage treatment processes for small communities is marketed under the generic heading of 'black box technology'. Within the range, individual models of plants are given names of mythical smaller people such as IMP, ELF, SPRITE and PIXIE. Marketers now have opportunities to be really creative in promoting these technologies.

This lateral thinking has helped technical innovation to inform business innovation. Anglian have now begun to join forces with other companies to develop local sewage treatment and recycling projects in new housing estates. This helps to cut drinking water consumption and bills, but also opens up the prospect of competition. Anglian Water formed a joint venture with Beaker, the house developer, opening their first new estate in the north west of England.

Anglian have also created partnerships with academic institutions. Because they have strong technology needs, Anglian have linked up with Imperial College (London), Cranfield, Cambridge, Trondheim and the University of New South Wales. Staff of Anglian Water are lecturers in these universities. Anglian provides operational projects and site visits for MSc courses and sponsors research assistants and PhDs. The benefit to Anglian Water, apart from an extension to its knowledge assets and resources, has been some excellent research.

TENSIONS AND PARADOXES – SOME FINAL THOUGHTS

Water utilities are well placed to act as laboratories for creativity, innovation and knowledge creation. Anglian's progress demonstrates what can be achieved with positive leadership. The Anglian Water learning management system recognizes the importance of self-managing teams and groups. It encourages mind opening as well as skills endowment. Our experience of creating the University of Water has made Anglian aware of a number of important tensions and paradoxes that organizations must embrace if they are truly to grow as learning organizations.

The long-term prospects of an individual and the company must be bound together. Staff who feel valued will stay longer. The corporate university is a flag around which we can all proudly gather and see a bright future. It needs to be founded on good communication of knowledge and best practice. An intranet is a tool, not an end. Vocational development should apply to all employees and should not be restricted to skills. Vocational development is not just for non-academic workers! The university provides integrated learning rather than fragmented learning. It allows the company to develop as a distinct entity, drawing on the strengths of transient individuals. The individuals and organization both get progressively smarter.

Organizational identity is strengthened through diversity. The University of Water's federal structure allows others to join readily. As Anglian win new contracts, they continue to restructure operations; new organizations can join without straining the identity of the university as a whole. Indeed, the group will come to benefit greatly from such diversity.

A learning organization is a physical structure and an idea. The University of Water exists both in real form and in the mind. It is linked to the operating company of Anglian Water through each individual. It exists both in the tangible and physical form of the learning assets provided by the company, and in the intellectual, behavioural and cultural attitudes of each individual. The employees *are* the learning organization.

What gets measured gets done – and the most important aspects

---

In any learning organization, of course, there are many day-to-day tensions to be managed.

- Delivering now vs future promise.
- Stimulation of interest and expectation vs managing expectation and avoiding disappointment.
- Abstract conceptual framework vs commonplace working language and practice.
- Focused vs spontaneous and hence 'chaotic' change.
- Mixing established and new employees.
- Overload vs invisibility.
- Structure vs flexibility and innovative freedom.
- Coping with the 'day job' and learning at the same time.
- Employee retention vs 'new blood'.
- Commercial vs social issues.
- Buttons vs levers.

of learning cannot be measured. In simple terms, we know we must do more and spend less. But how to measure commitment, knowledge or happiness? The issue of the measurement of learning is fascinating. Measuring learning by bottom-line benefits is probably impossible: the outcomes are simply too far down the line. We measure an athlete's success in terms of speed and place. But, I ask myself, what measurements justify an athlete training for races? Surely it is self-evident that untrained, lazy people are not likely to be Olympic champions. Commitment to learning is usually an act of faith. Leaders must commit to their staff's learning in the same way parents commit to their children's education.

Inner response to change can affect change itself. There is a tension between the will/will not and the can/cannot people in an organization.

ATTITUDE TENSIONS

	Will	**Will not**
Can	Able	Cynical
Cannot	Willing	Dysfunctional

- Able people – the 'will-can' people – are to be prized and nurtured.
- Willing people – the 'will-cannot' people – need help and support and to be given the right skills.
- Cynical people – the 'will not, but can' – may have to go, as they are likely to be disruptive.
- Dysfunctional people – the 'will not and cannot'– will certainly have to leave: their inability to cope means they may need sympathetic handling during their exit.

Understanding people's inner responses to change is vitally important. For example, a complaint of initiative overload may be a smokescreen for resistance to change. New people may want to change what they inherit just to make their own mark on the business process, rather than to improve it. Understanding psychology is very important. When I started I would not have imagined that I would say that! But a manager must understand what emotional buttons are likely to be activated in individuals driving change, and what levers can be pulled to encourage change.

Learning demands both order and disorder. Order is that aspect of the business that imposes rigour: creating stable operational structures, planning, setting objectives derived from business plans, maintaining processes, and so on. Disorder is the much more chaotic, opportunistic, creative process of the entrepreneur. Are these different phases in an organization (see Phased Growth Model diagram below)? Can they be contained together, with one more dominant at different times, as shown in the Dual Growth Model diagram overleaf?

PHASED GROWTH MODEL

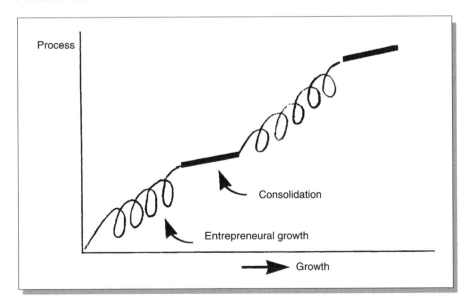

DUAL GROWTH MODEL

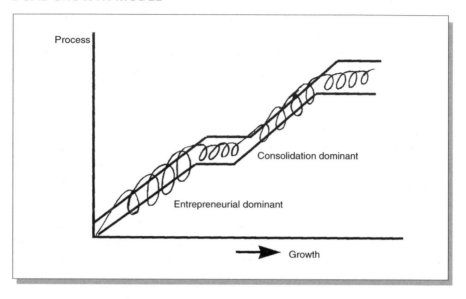

In both of these cases, order and disorder enjoy productive synergy and co-existence. An organization's own view of its growth can be somewhat inaccurate. Sometimes there is post-event rationalization; what felt chaotic at the time is later explained by patterns of events invisible – or even non-existent – at the time.

Growth may come from entrepreneurial chaos or consolidating stability. The Dual Growth Model shows the greatest growth during the dominance of innovative entrepreneurialism. In my view, long-term growth is likely to come from an alternation between the different dominant phases. If an organization is stuck in one phase all the time, its growth will eventually crash. The chaotic phase may be much more organic, *ad hoc*, with much greater, even explosive, energy and activity. But the risks to organizational stability are high. Leaders must give intellectual and even physical space for creativity to be nurtured and exploited, and take care to preserve what's best of the organization itself – that's wise management! Applying chaos theory – as developed, for example, by Ralph Stacey of the University of Hertford in the UK – may be helpful in managing turbulent times.

In the case of Anglian Water, with its commitment to the stability demanded of a public service, we tended to have consolidation dominant for a greater time than entrepreneurial activity, but even that is an over-simplification. It may be better to think of entrepreneurial dominance in the concession-seeking commercial subsidiaries and consolidation dominance in the operational subsidiaries. Customers will want the reassurance of long-term stability in operational contracts. Could we think of an organization having the stability of explicit or recorded information, expressed as best practice and quality assurance manuals, alongside the energy of tacit experimentation and creativity?

The process of innovation, which is the exploitation of creativity, is the bridge to the more structured character of an organization. Indeed, innovation can be viewed as the glue in a well balanced organization and is a function of wise management. Tacit learning and knowledge can be viewed as a living envelope that changes shape and size with time.

Corporate entrepreneurs are vital to an organization's success, but are difficult to manage. A successful global water company must have corporate entrepreneurs co-existing with career lifers providing operational stability.

The very essence of the learning organization is ambiguity. Managing such an organization is the business of facing and living with dilemmas. But then, all of nature is paradoxical. Understanding this fundamental fact, perhaps, is the foundation of wisdom.

In the knowledge economy, nobody has the opportunity to opt out. Employers have a special responsibility to provide opportunities to learn. And they must be continuously available: our learning needs to be refreshed constantly. Every organization will have moments of baffling stupidity; but we must use these as learning experiences. An innovative, wise organization only makes new mistakes.

Learning awakens a deep consciousness in people. To modify Descartes: I learn, therefore I am. We should encourage employees to ask not only what learning can do for them, but also what they can do for learning. To answer the question posed in the title: Yes, wise people do make good innovators. They are often the best!

Afterword

What have we learnt on this journey of exploration? We have looked at the landscape of creativity and innovation from a number of perspectives. We have been particularly interested in how to *organize* for innovation. We are working in a global economy, increasingly complicated and uncertain. At such a point in our history, innovation has become too important an activity to be left to the maverick entrepreneur. In every sector of the economy – commercial, public, not-for-profit – we need to learn how we might innovate together, both within organizations and in the increasingly complicated networks between them.

We have seen that innovation is at the heart of what it means to be human. It exploits our abilities to collaborate, learn and create. By innovating, we have progressed from cave paintings to digital cameras, from flint tools to computers – and from multi-part hunting tools to intercontinental missiles. Innovation is a perilous activity; all too often, it generates more problems than it solves. It proceeds in an endless spiral from problems to solutions, and from solutions to more complex problems that demand ever more innovative solutions. We have also found that innovation is at least as much a *social* phenomenon as a technological one, and that many of the most significant innovations have been cultural and social rather than scientific or technical.

We have learnt that innovation doesn't happen everywhere, all the time. Certain conditions seem to be necessary for people to innovate, and establishing the environment, the 'culture' of innovation – either between or within organizations – is complex and can be fraught with difficulties.

We have learnt that the process of innovation can be systematized inside organizations – indeed, must be systematized if it is to survive. The processes themselves may be reasonably simple or extremely complex; but they must be clearly understood by everyone involved if they are to be successful. The process must be managed with a care for different priorities and values in the innovating teams; the 'hard' elements of measurement, evaluation and control must be balanced by a proper respect for people's creativity and the feelings that go with it. We have also seen how innovation teams have their own life and their own rules.

We have learnt that innovation often proceeds not in simple straight lines but in cycles or spirals. What has been learnt in one phase of innovation can easily be lost in later stages, and it is vital to capture unused ideas, failures or undeveloped opportunities so that we might return to them later. We innovate in uncertain environments – indeed, innovation often itself generates uncertainty. The future is increasingly unpredictable, and we cannot afford to waste what we have learnt.

We have discovered that we can learn to increase our capacity to create. But we must recognize that creativity is a special kind of activity, following its own rules and making its own demands. Training is helpful, but must be seen as part of a wider strategy to foster creativity within organizations. And we have learnt that knowledge must be managed for innovation; not merely as a resource but as a dynamic. We must find ways of harnessing what people know and encouraging them to share it. We must work to develop knowledge towards the wisdom that informs the highest creativity.

PLAYING THE PARADOX – BALANCING LOCAL KNOWLEDGE AND CENTRAL CONTROL IN INNOVATION

A recent survey has once again highlighted the need to view innovation as a multi-disciplinary activity.

Innovation Exchange, a forum based at the London Business School, set out to identify best and worst practices, and the future challenges facing organizations intending to pursue an innovation strategy. The team conducted 41 interviews in 21 member organizations in the UK, between October 2000 and January 2001.

The survey covered four broad areas: leadership, culture, strategy and vision, and processes. The study team discovered anecdotal evidence that innovation is all too often poorly managed. Again and again, they heard remarks such as 'Innovation in this company is not really wanted'; 'New product development is something we worry about if we don't have anything else to do'; or 'Innovation is someone else's job'.

The team found that leadership is critical to innovation success. Participants stressed the need for such leadership to be consistent across the organization, and well communicated. Successful leaders encourage experiment and tolerate failure. They connect emotionally as well as rationally with innovators in their organizations.

Leadership is part of a larger culture. Participants characterized an innovative culture as encompassing fun, focus, freedom to fail and flexibility. It is results-oriented and team-based, with an appetite for learning and an ability to kill off projects quickly without damage or ill feeling. In creating such a culture, many companies face the difficulty of historical differences of culture between divisions and business units.

A coherent strategy, too, was seen as crucial. Centralization was a key element in the innovation strategies of many of the companies participating in the survey. Strategy was driven, again and again, by merger and acquisition activities; companies were looking to innovation to provide the 'glue' to stimulate more organic growth in the future. In order to streamline operations, make them more efficient and reap benefits of economies of scale, companies are centralizing innovation; portfolios are shrinking and 'megabrands' are emerging.

As a consequence, companies are seeking to manage innovation globally. Future challenges for strategy are:

- leading the change effectively and still achieving the output;
- ensuring everyone can link their job to the company's vision and strategy;
- defining roles of business units and the centre;
- finding the right balance between management and control;
- motivating those that do not work on 'megabrands'.

The processes of innovation present a number of important challenges. Participants stressed the need to see innovation processes as a means, not an end, and to set meaningful targets within them. Innovation processes need to be appropriate to the company's situation and clearly linked to an overall strategy. Finding the right processes might take time and experiment. The study found that, on the whole, idea generation as such does not seem to be a problem. The problem is generating and identifying the 'right' ideas early on. Resources are wasted by not killing projects early enough. Incidentally, suggestion schemes do not seem to deliver the desired results: ideas that can be usefully taken forward. The challenges for these processes in the future are:

- developing mechanisms that enable identification of the really big ideas early on;
- finding or developing the tools that enable making the great leaps as well as the small improvements;
- developing the discipline to liberate resources without disrupting existing business.

Overall, the study team found a central paradox facing those seeking to manage organizational innovation. Companies seem to be facing the same paradox: balancing local knowledge with central control.

Grasping hold of innovation is like trying to grasp the proverbial snake. Innovation is indeed an alchemical activity, involving many different areas of organizational life and expertise. But the final point is surely just this: that it is an *activity*.

The great danger is that we might be seduced into thinking of innovation as a *thing*: a good to be gained, rather than an activity to be pursued. Many areas of management fall prey to this syndrome. If only we can define it, name it as an object, perhaps we might be able to capture it, control it – and say that our organization has it. 'Quality', 'empowerment', 'strategy' – all are words that we use in this desperate attempt to grasp what cannot be held.

Therapists know this condition well; they call it **nominalization**. To nominalize is to transform a verb (or adjective) into a noun. Nominalization creates a kind of illusory object in the mind, entrancing us with the false hope that 'it' can somehow be grasped, touched, bought or otherwise possessed. Action becomes petrified into an object, and we become victims of a delusion.

Nominalization is signalled in many of our old stories. King Midas becomes obsessed with gold and turns everything he loves into dead metal; Sleeping Beauty falls asleep, and all the castle with her, through the workings of an evil fairy seeking to impose her will, and is awoken only by the power of love. In therapy, nominalization can focus the patient's mind on an impossible dream, paralysing action where it is most necessary. In organizational life, nominalization can create magic formulas that seduce managers into pursuing grand strategic projects that promise much but deliver little. We become hypnotized by the word: the language of nominalization casts its spell and means are transformed into ends. Most of the 'fads that forgot people' are expressed in nominalized terms: 'total quality'; 'business process reengineering'; 'customer relationship management'. Innovation can too easily become another such magical formula – particularly as it tends to be associated with technology, the creation of new objects and machines. We run the danger, like King Midas, of mistaking gold for the process of creating wealth, of mistaking the innovative product for the process of innovation.

Breaking the spell means *denominalizing*. We should ask, not what we want, but what we want *to do*. The real question is not 'How do we start?' It is a more fundamental question, and one that we must ask ourselves continually if the spark of innovation is to catch in our organizations. This is the question where the alchemy of innovation begins: What do you want to create?

Bibliography

Anderson, Harold. *Creativity and its Cultivation*. Harper and Brothers Publishers, 1959.

Battram, Arthur. *Navigating Complexity*. The Industrial Society, 1998.

Claxton, Guy. *Hare Brain, Tortoise Mind*. Fourth Estate, 1997.

de Bono, Edward. *Lateral Thinking for Management*. Penguin Books, 1990.

Drucker, Peter. *Innovation and Entrepreneurship*. Heinemann, 1985.

Dyson, James. *Against the Odds*. Texere Publishing, 2000.

Fritz, Robert. *Corporate Tides*. Berrett-Koehler, 1996.

Fritz, Robert. *Creating*. Fawcett Columbine, 1991.

Fritz, Robert. *The Path of Least Resistance*. Fawcett Columbine, 1984.

Gardner, Howard. *Creating Minds*. Basic Books, 1993.

Hall, Peter. *Cities in Civilization*. Weidenfeld and Nicolson, 1998.

Hammer, Michael and Champy, James. *Reengineering the Corporation*. Nicholas Brealey Publishing, 1993.

Henry, Jane [ed]. *Creative Management*. Sage Publications Ltd, 1991.

Henry, Jane and Walker, David [eds]. *Managing Innovation*. Sage Publications Ltd, 1991.

Huizinga, Johan. *Homo Ludens*. The Beacon Press, 1950.

Jung, Carl *Man and his Symbols*. Dell Publishing Co, 1968

Koestler, Arthur. *The Act of Creation*. Hutchinson, 1966.

Mithen, Steven. *The Prehistory of the Mind*. Thames and Hudson, 1999.

Nolan, Vincent. *The Innovator's Handbook*. Sphere Books, 1989.

Nonaka, Ikujiro and Takeuchi, Hirotaka. *The Knowledge-creating Company.* Oxford University Press, 1995.

Ortega y Gasset, José. *Phenomenology and Art.* Norton, 1975.

Rickards, Tudor. *Creativity and Problem Solving at Work.* Gower, 1988.

Rickards, Tudor. *Creativity and the Management of Change.* Blackwell Publishers Ltd, 1999.

Scarborough, Harry, Swan, Jacky and Preston, John. *Knowledge Management: a literature review.* Institute of Personnel and Development, 1999.

Senge, Peter. *The Fifth Discipline.* Random House Business Books, 1993.

Syrett, Michel and Lammiman, Jean. *Managing Live Innovation.* Butterworth-Heinemann, 1998.

Young, Trevor. *The Handbook of Project Management.* Kogan Page, 1998.

Index